Holding Fast to Grace

Holding Fast to Grace

Roy L. Aldrich

Grace Gospel Press
Milwaukee, Wisconsin

Holding Fast to Grace, by Roy L. Aldrich. Originally published: Dunham Publishing Company, Findlay, Ohio, 1962.

ISBN: 978-0-9799637-3-5

Grace Gospel Press
10328 W. Oklahoma Ave.
Milwaukee, WI 53227
U.S.A.
www.gracegospelpress.com

Printed in the United States of America

ACKNOWLEDGMENT

Grateful acknowledgment is made to the many authors and publishers who have graciously given permission to quote selections from their materials in this book. The list is too long to reproduce here. However, I would especially urge readers to secure and read the books on the spiritual life which are quoted in chapter 1, "Walking with the Lord under Grace." These books have been a great personal blessing to me, and I am glad to recommend them to all who seek a closer walk with the Lord.

CONTENTS

FOREWORD

One of the decisive questions in Biblical interpretation is the proper understanding of the meaning and relationship of law and grace. Dr. Aldrich with unusual insight and thorough scholarship has supplied a penetrating analysis of this important subject which is faithful to the Scriptures and will do much to dispel the confusion that often exists in these important aspects of Biblical revelation.

JOHN F. WALVOORD
President, Dallas Theological Seminary

PREFACE

Holding Fast to Grace is a critical study of law and grace with emphasis upon the positive side of the life under grace. The first chapter, entitled "Walking with the Lord under Grace," contains quotations from many standard spiritual life and devotional books which explain the method of living a deeper Christian life. It is shown that the Bible pattern for spirituality is to consciously and continuously realize the presence of Christ.

This chapter is logically the conclusion of the book but it has been placed first for these reasons: (1) to show that freedom from the Mosaic law is as far from antinomianism (lawlessness) as the heavens are from the earth, (2) in order that the critical study of law and grace may be considered in the light of the blessing of fellowship with Christ. No one will miss Moses, with his tables of stone, if he walks with the Lord—the Man of grace.

INTRODUCTION

The most persistent and widespread and deadly error of all Bible history is legalism. The natural mind has an affinity for legalism and corresponding disaffection for grace. The multitudes prefer to spend their money and labor in a vain attempt to merit what God declares can be secured only "without money and without price" (Isa. 55:1, 2).

The believer, saved through grace, is God's masterwork. This is the teaching of Ephesians 2:1-10. "For we are his workmanship (masterwork), created in Christ Jesus unto good works, which God hath before ordained that we should walk in them" (Eph. 2:10).

On the other hand Satan's masterwork consists of those deceived by his systems of self-righteousness. "And no marvel; for Satan himself is transformed into an angel of light. Therefore it is no great thing if his ministers also be transformed as the ministers of righteousness; whose end shall be according to their works" (2 Cor. 11:14, 15). Israel, with all of her light, followed this path of deception: "For they being ignorant of God's righteousness, and going about to establish their own righteousness, have not submitted themselves unto the righteousness of God" (Rom. 10:3).

But those who are saved by grace are not automatically delivered from legalism. The old nature, with its affinity for a merit system, still remains. The Galatian Christians were saved by grace but later entangled in dangerous forms of Mosaic legalism. "Are you so foolish? having begun in the Spirit, are ye now made perfect by the flesh?" (Gal. 3:3).

It is probably true that no believer is without some taint of legalism. It is more certain that no one fully comprehends the grace of God. Isaiah declares that God's willingness to "abundantly pardon" sin is as different from our thoughts about this matter as the heavens are higher than the earth (Isa. 55:7-9). But all of this does not free us from the obligation to understand what we can about the grace of God, for only to the extent that we apprehend grace are we safe from legalism.

In the following pages we shall show that the believer is free from every aspect of the law of Moses including the Ten Commandments. Some will consider this such rank heresy that they will read no further. However, if the language of the New Testament is to be taken at its face value, such a conclusion is not only inevitable but it is the only position that avoids contradictions and inconsistencies.

Chapter 1

WALKING WITH THE LORD UNDER GRACE

The New Testament teaches with emphasis that both justification and sanctification are apart from the law. It is in the context of Paul's great treatise on sanctification in Romans that he declares, "For sin shall not have dominion over you: for ye are not under the law, but under grace" (Rom. 6:14). Although this verse has its problems, it clearly teaches that freedom from the power of sin is dependent upon freedom from the law and subjection to grace.

In Galatians, the great charter of Christian liberty, Paul equates the "works of the law" to the energy of the flesh: "This only would I learn of you, received ye the Spirit by the works of the law. or by the hearing of faith? Are ye so foolish? having begun in the Spirit, are ye now made perfect by the flesh?" (Gal. 3:2, 3). In other words, to try to live by the law would be as foolish as to think that salvation came by the law. It must be acknowledged that the Spirit was received by faith and it should be recognized that He continues to work in the believer only on this same principle.

Later in this same epistle Paul explains in greater detail the meaning of living by the Spirit and not by the flesh:

> But I say, walk and live habitually in the (Holy) Spirit—responsive to and controlled and guided by the Spirit, then you will not gratify the cravings and desires of the flesh—of human nature without God.
>
> For the desires of the flesh are opposed to the Holy) Spirit, and the (desires of the) Spirit are opposed to the flesh (godless human nature); for these are antagonistic to each other—continually withstanding and in conflict with each other—so that you are not free but are prevented from doing what you desire to do.
>
> But if you are guided (led) by the (Holy) Spirit you are not subject to the law (Gal. 5:16-18. The Amplified New Testament).

In Colossians the spiritual Christian life is described as walking in Christ: "As ye have therefore received Christ Jesus the Lord, so walk ye in Him" (Col. 2:6). To "walk in (or by) the Spirit" refers to the same experience as "walking in Christ." The meaning and relationship of the two expressions are brought together in this passage: "But we all, with unveiled face beholding as in a mirror the glory of the Lord, are transformed into the same image from glory to glory, even as from the Lord the Spirit" (2 Cor. 3:18 R.V.). As the believer is occupied with the Lord he is changed by the power of the Spirit into the image of Christ.

"Perhaps it will be asked," writes Professor Godet, "what is the connection between the passages in which our sanctification is attributed to the Holy Spirit and those in which it is attributed to Christ Himself living in us?" (Gal. 2:20).

"The answer is easy. In reality these two classes of expression refer to one and the same fact. What is the work of the Holy Spirit? It is to impart Christ to us, with everything that is His, and to make Him live again in us, as the grain of wheat which lies dead in the earth is made by the power of nature to live again in each of the grains in the ear."[1]

It simplifies our understanding of the spiritual life to realize that the various expressions used to describe it refer only to different aspects of the same experience. To "walk in the Spirit," to "walk in Christ," to "walk with the Lord," to "abide in Christ," and to "look unto Jesus," all refer to the same thing.

The story of Hudson Taylor's entrance into the more abundant Christian life is told in the book, *Hudson Taylor's Spiritual Secret*, by Dr. and Mrs. Howard Taylor. This small volume cannot be recommended too highly. The chapter entitled "The Exchanged Life" tells the story of Mr. Taylor's great transformation. Hudson Taylor had been a missionary in China for a number of years before he learned the secret that changed his whole life. The light finally dawned as the result of a letter received from a fellow missionary, John McCarthy, who was laboring

---

[1] Evan Hopkins, *The Law of Liberty in the Spiritual Life*, American Rights are held by The Sunday School Times Company, p. 73.

in another part of China. McCarthy wrote about the way of holiness. His entire letter should be read, but its essence is contained in this quotation from a book called *Christ is All*: "The Lord Jesus received is holiness begun; the Lord Jesus cherished is holiness advancing; the Lord Jesus counted upon as never absent would be holiness complete."[2] The writer has found it profitable to memorize and meditate upon the last part of this quotation and strongly recommends this to the reader. "THE LORD JESUS COUNTED UPON AS NEVER ABSENT WOULD BE HOLINESS COMPLETE."

This truth transformed the life of Hudson Taylor. He entered "the exchanged life" of "no longer I," but "Christ liveth in me." He learned that abiding, not striving and struggling, was the secret of joy and power. It was this experience, this new apprehension of the sufficiency of Christ for everything, that ushered Hudson Taylor into his great life of spiritual power and missionary accomplishment.

Mr. Taylor discovered something new for himself, but something as old as the Bible. Enoch knew and practiced this secret: "And Enoch walked with God: and he was not; for God took him" (Gen. 5:24). David counted upon the presence of the Lord in his severest trials and greatest triumphs: "Seek the Lord and his strength, seek his presence continually" (I Chron. 16:11; Ps. 105:4). Paul said, "For me to live is Christ" (Phil. 1:21). Brother Lawrence called this secret "the practice of the presence of God."

---

[2] Dr. and Mrs. Howard Taylor, *Hudson Taylor's Spiritual Secret*, China Inland Mission, p. 111.

It is the will of God that every believer should live this life of closest fellowship with the Lord. The great classic challenge and invitation to such a life of dedication and transformation (Rom. 12:1, 2) closes with the assurance that this is the only gateway into "that good, and acceptable, and perfect will of God." Hannah W. Smith has eloquently described the blessing of living in this "perfect will of God":

> Better and sweeter than health, or friends, or money or fame or ease or prosperity is the adorable will of God. It gilds the darkest hours with a divine halo and sheds brightest sunshine on the gloomiest paths. He always reigns who has made it his kingdom, and nothing can go amiss to him.[3]

Granted that the dedicated Christian life is blessed and desirable, but can it actually be experienced by so simple a formula as "always counting on the presence of the Lord"? Yes, if the expression is really understood. It means that Christ should be as real to us as the presence of those with whom we associate each day. Of course he is not known through our physical senses, but His presence should be just as real as though we could see and touch Him. We walk with the Lord by faith, but the very function of faith is to make real the things that are not seen (Heb. 11:1). Alexander MacLaren has emphasized this aspect of Christian experience with his usual insight and clarity:

> Let me say in the plainest, simplest, strongest way I can, that the dwelling of Christ in the believing heart is to

---

[3] Hannah W. Smith, *The Christian's Secret of a Happy Life*, Fleming H. Revell Co., p. 51.

be regarded as being a plain, literal fact. . . . It is not to be weakened down into any notion of participation in His likeness, following His example or the like. A dead Plato may so influence his followers, but that is not how a living Christ influences His disciples. . . . This indwelling may be a permanent and unbroken one. . . . Oh! What a contrast to that idea of a perpetual unbroken inhabitation of Jesus in our spirit and to our consciousness is presented by our ordinary life! We might with unbroken blessedness possess Him in our hearts and instead we have only visits short and far between. God means and wishes that Christ may continuously dwell in our hearts. Does He to your own consciousness dwell in yours?[4]

This truth of the real presence of Christ is not new nor original, but is the core and climax of the great spiritual life and devotional books which have been most widely used to instruct and bless the people of God. The authors have used their own style and illustrations—but actually they agree in reducing all the mysteries and complexities of the abundant Christian life to the simplicity of walking with the Lord. The reader is urged to consider carefully and prayerfully the following quotations and see their agreement in this one great essential:

I have quitted all forms of devotions and set prayers but those to which my state obliges me. And I make it my business only to persevere in His holy presence, wherein I keep myself by a simple attention, and a general fond

---

[4] Quoted from Oswald J. Sanders, *Christ Indwelling and Enthroned*, Christian Literature Crusade, p. 26

regard to God, which I may call an actual presence of God; or, to speak better, an habitual, silent, and secret conversation of the soul with God, which often causes me joys and raptures inwardly, and sometimes also outwardly, so great that I am forced to use means to moderate them and prevent their appearance to others . . . I will send you one of these books, which treat of the presence of God, a subject which, in my opinion, contains the whole spiritual life; and it seems to me that whoever duly practices it will soon become spiritual.[5]

True spirituality is a reality. It is all of the manifestations of the Spirit in and through the one in whom He dwells. He manifests in the believer the life which is Christ. He came not to reveal Himself but to make Christ real to the heart, and through the heart of man. Thus the Apostle Paul could write: "For this cause I bow my knees unto the Father of our Lord Jesus Christ, of whom the whole family in heaven and earth is named, that he would grant you, according to the riches of his glory to be strengthened with might by his Spirit in the inner man; that Christ may dwell in your hearts by faith; that ye, being rooted and grounded in love, may be able to comprehend with all saints what is the breadth, and length, and depth, and height; and to know the love of Christ, which passeth knowledge, that ye might be filled with all the fulness of God."[6]

---

[5] Brother Lawrence, *The Practice of the Presence of God*, Fleming H. Revell Co., pp. 36, 37, 45.

[6] Lewis Sperry Chafer, *He That Is Spiritual*, Dunham Publishing Co., p. 185.

Too often we fail to get to the place of self-confessed defeat, where we cry out, "I can't!" and own, "O wretched man that I am! Who shall deliver me?" (Rom. 7:24). But there is scant hope of believing "He does" till we cry out the double confession: "I can't, but He can!" Not until we see that we live the Christian life in exactly the same way we began the Christian life; namely by looking away completely from our own selves, and fastening our faith solely upon the resources and the power of God. Not until we do this will the victory be ours! . . . Thus the Christian life is Christ. He is not only the center and source of our life. He is our life (Col. 3:4). As we believe He is what He is to us, and we are what we are in Him, His own radiant, joyous, triumphant resurrection life is manifested in our experience. This is normal Christianity. This, and nothing less than this, is the Christian life, nurtured, sustained and manifested by faith in the Son of God.[7]

It is the great secret, a secret which has been to me, oh so wonderful. A very many years ago I came to Him burdened with guilt and fear; I took that simple secret, and it took away all my fear and sin. Years passed on, and I found sin overcame me, and my temptations were too strong for me. I came to Him a second time, and He whispered to me, "Christ in you," and I had victory, rest, and such sweet blessing ever since.[8]

But when I know and practice the secret of release, I inwardly take my stand of faith, "I have been crucified

---

[7] Merrill F. Unger, *Pathways to Power*, Zondervan Publishing House, pp. 62, 64.

[8] Oswald J. Sanders, op cit., p. 26.

with Christ." I say to Satan, "I am not here to respond. I am dead and buried with Christ." And as I say that, another realization will rise within me: "Christ liveth in me." It will be as the child said, "when Satan knocks at the door, I send Jesus to answer it." . . . The moment I realize His presence I am free. My heart has a counter-attraction, greater than the attraction of the temptation. My love for Him, my joy in Him cancels out the contrary pull. The more we live in Gal. 2:20, in the consciousness of the relationship it describes, the more we have a steady shield of defence in daily temptation, and the more accustomed we become to the natural use of it, "the shield of faith wherewith ye shall be able to quench all the fiery darts of the wicked."[9]

Now let it be understood and constantly borne in mind, that this self-renunciation and taking hold on Christ as our strength, is not a mere speculation, an opinion, an article of faith, a profession, but must be one of the most practical realities in the world. It must become to the mind an omnipresent reality, insomuch that you shall no more attempt anything in your own strength than a man who never could walk without crutches would attempt to arise and walk without thinking of them. To such a one his crutches become a part of himself. They are his legs. He as naturally uses them as we do the members of our body. He no more forgets them, or attempts to walk without them than we attempt to walk without our feet. Now just so it is with one who spiritually understands his dependence

---

[9] Norman Grubb, *The Liberating Secret*, Christian Literature Crusade, pp. 119, 120.

on Christ. He knows he can walk, and that he must walk but he as naturally uses the strength of Christ in all his duties as the lame man uses his crutches. It is really an omnipresent reality to him that he must lean upon Christ as it is to the lame man that he must lean upon his crutches. He learns on all occasions to keep hold of the strength of Christ and does not even think of doing anything without Him. He knows that he need not attempt anything in his own strength; and that if he should, it will result in failure and disgrace, just as really and as well as the man without feet or legs knows that for him to attempt to walk without his crutch would ensure a fall. This is a great, and I fear, a rarely learned lesson with professed Christians, and yet how strange that it should be so, since, in every instance, attempts to walk without Christ have resulted in complete and instantaneous, failure. All profess to know their own weakness, and their remedy, and yet how few give evidence of knowing either.[10]

Now my thesis is this: we have been operating upon a false basis. We have conceived of the Christian life as an imitation of Christ. It is not an imitation of Christ. It is a participation of Christ. "For we are made partakers of Christ" (Heb. 3:14). There are good things in Thomas A. Kempis' *Imitation of Christ,* but the basic idea is false to the principles that underlie the Christian life. To proceed on the basis of imitation will plunge us in just the sort of slough of despond Paul found himself in when he wrote Romans 7.[11]

---

[10] Charles G. Finney, *Sanctification*, Christian Literature Crusade, pp. 77, 78.
[11] Quoted from F. J. Huegel, *Bone of His Bone*, Zondervan Publishing

I feel simply carried along each hour, doing my part in a plan which is far beyond myself. This sense of cooperation with God in little things is what so astonishes me, for I never have felt it this way before. I need something, and turn round to find it waiting for me. I must work, to be sure, but there is God working along with me. To know this gives a sense of security and assurance for the future which is also new to my life. I seem to have to make sure of only one thing now, and every other thing "takes care of itself," or I prefer to say what is more true, God takes care of all the rest. My part is to live this hour in continuous inner conversation with God and in perfect responsiveness to His will to make this hour gloriously rich. This seems to be all I need to think about. . . . Any hour of any day may be made perfect by merely choosing. It is perfect if one looks toward God that entire hour, waiting for His leadership all through the hour and trying hard to do every tiny thing exactly as God wishes it done, as perfectly as possible. No emotions are necessary. Just the doing of God's will perfectly makes the hour a perfect one. And the results of that one perfect hour, I believe, will echo down through eternity. . . . O, this thing of keeping in constant touch with God, of making Him the object of my thought and the companion of my conversations, is the most amazing thing I ever ran across. It is working. I cannot do it even half of a day—not yet, but I believe I shall be doing it some day for the entire day. It is a matter of acquiring a new habit of thought. Now I like God's presence so much that when for a half hour or so He slips out of mind—as He does many times a day—I

House, p. 19.

feel as though I had deserted Him, and as though I had lost something very precious in my life.[12]

Jesus loved the Father, and there is no difficulty in giving up the self-life when you are in love with the living Christ. The thing for us to do therefore is, not to dwell on the crucifixion, on the giving-up side, but to allow our whole nature to be drawn to the living Christ—not to death, but life. Moreover, seek that abounding life which makes it so easy to say No to self. Make the living Jesus the reality of your whole life. Go about saying, "I live, yet not I, but Christ liveth in me."[13]

Think what it is we really possess, if Christ is in us. It was no mere figure of speech that the apostle employed when he declared that Christ was living in him. And what was true of him may be equally true of us. What then is it we possess? We have Him, in whom all fullness of life actually dwells, in whom infinite resources are stored up for our use. Everything needed for continual growth, for perpetual freshness, and for abundant fruitfulness are found in Him. All power, all grace, all purity, and all fulness, absolutely everything to make all grace abound toward us, in us, and through us, are stored up in Him who verily dwells within us.[14]

Looking unto Jesus—and not at the brightness of our joy, the strength of our assurance, or the warmth of our love! Otherwise, when for a little time this love seems to

---

[12] Frank C. Laubach, *Letters By a Modern Mystic*, Fleming H. Revell Co., pp. 12, 19, 23.

[13] F. B. Meyer, *Meet For The Master's Use*, Moody Press, p. 103.

[14] Evan Hopkins, op cit., p. 77.

have grown cold, this assurance to have vanished, this joy to have failed us—either as the result of our own faithlessness, or for the trial of our faith—immediately, having lost our feelings, we think that we have lost our strength, and we allow ourselves to fall into an abyss of sorrow, even into cowardly idleness, or perhaps sinful complaints. Ah! rather let us remember that if the feelings with their sweetness, are absent, the faith with its strength remains with us. To be able always to be "abounding in the work of the Lord" (I Cor. 15:58) let us look steadily, not at our ever changeful hearts, but at Jesus, who is always the same . . . Looking unto Jesus—and not our defeats or victories. If we look at our defeats we shall be cast down; if we look at our victories we shall be puffed up. And neither will help us to fight the good fight of faith (1 Tim. 6:12). Like all our blessings, the victory, with the faith which wins it, is the gift of God through our Lord Jesus Christ (1 Cor. 15:57) and to Him is all the glory.[15]

Looking unto Jesus—and not at our faith. The last device of the adversary, when he cannot make us look elsewhere, is to turn our eyes from our Saviour to our faith, and thus to discourage us if it is weak, to fill us with pride if it is strong: and either way to weaken us. For power does not come from the faith, but from the Saviour by faith. It is not looking at our look, it is "looking unto Jesus."[16]

---

[15] Theodore Monad, *Looking Unto Jesus*, Box 351, Athens, Georgia, pp. 18, 20.
[16] Theodore Monad, Ibid., pp. 20, 21.

In Galatians 5:16, 17, we have these words: "This I say then, walk in the Spirit, and ye shall not fulfill the lust of the flesh, For the flesh lusteth against the Spirit and the Spirit against the flesh; and these are contrary the one to the other: so that ye cannot do the things that ye would." The presence of the flesh, and of its lusting in the believing man is here recognized. The remedy is, not its annihilation, not its change of nature; but the same as in Romans 8—the practical fellowship of the soul with a personal Christ, by walking in the Spirit. And the promise is, that if I walk in the Spirit i.e., let the Holy Spirit have His way with me, in revealing Christ to my soul through the scriptures, and yielding myself to God in obedience to the Word, as the Word reveals His will, "I shall not fulfill the lusts of the flesh," for "I cannot do the things that I would." The things that I would do are the things that would gratify the flesh. But if I am in real communion with God, I cannot do these things. The consciousness of His displeasure, to which a soul walking in the Spirit becomes more and more sensitive, is a cause of such grief and unhappiness that, above all things, we shall dread the being overcome by sin; and in this communion with God we shall be kept by Him from the power of sin.[17]

Holiness is then a heart of pure love for God. It is Christ, our Sanctification, as life of our life. It is Christ, the Holy One in us, living, speaking, walking.[18]

January 31 . . . One does not surrender a life in an instant. That which is lifelong can only be surrendered in

---

[17] D. W. Whittle, *Life, Warfare and Victory*, Moody Press, pp. 86, 86.
[18] Ruth Paxson, *Rivers of Living Waters*, Moody Press, p. 34.

a lifetime. Nor is surrender to the will of God (per se) adequate to fullness of power in Christ. Maturity is the accomplishment of years, and I can only surrender to the will of God as I know what that will is. Hence, the fullness of the Spirit is not instantaneous but progressive, as I attain fullness of the Word, which reveals the will. If men were filled with the Spirit they would not write books on that subject, but on the Person whom the Spirit has come to reveal. Occupation with Christ is God's object.[19]

Then if we would please the indwelling Spirit we must be all taken up with Christ. The Spirit's present work is to honor Him, and everything He does has this for its ultimate purpose. And we must make our thoughts a clean sanctuary for His holy habitation. He dwells in our thoughts and soiled thoughts are as repugnant to Him as soiled linen to a king. Above all, we must have a cheerful faith that will keep on believing however radical the fluctuation in our emotional states may be . . . The Spirit indwelt life is not a special deluxe edition of Christianity to be enjoyed by a certain rare and privileged few who happen to be made of finer and more sensitive stuff than the rest. Rather, it is the normal state for every redeemed man and woman the world over. It is "that mystery which hath been hid from ages and from generations but now is made manifest to his saints: to whom God would make known what is the riches of the glory of this mystery among the gentiles, which is Christ in you, the hope of glory" (Col. 1:26). Faber,

---

[19] Elisabeth Elliot, *Shadow of the Almighty*, Harper and Brothers Publishers, p. 91.

in one of his sweet and reverent hymns, addressed this good word to the Holy Spirit:

> Ocean, wide flowing ocean,
> Thou, of uncreative Love;
> I tremble as within my soul
> I feel Thy waters move.[20]

As we begin to focus upon God the things of the Spirit will take shape before our inner eyes. Obedience to the word of Christ will bring an inward revelation of the Godhead (John 14:21-23). It will give acute perception enabling us to see God even as is promised to the pure in heart. A new God-consciousness will seize upon us and we shall begin to taste and hear and inwardly feel the God who is our life and our all. There will be seen the constant shining of the light that lighteth every man that cometh into the world. More and more, as our faculties grow sharper and more sure, God will become to us the great All, and His Presence the glory and wonder of our lives.[21]

Cultivate the consciousness of His presence. "Christ liveth in me." Paul knew it—knew it as a daily, practical fact. Since He is too deep down for feeling, we must do much consciously to realize His presence. Talk to Him. Recall His presence during the day. Especially would we urge the forming of this habit: Never rise from bed till you have assured yourself for the day, "Christ lives in me." . . . Adjust all your living to His presence. Set one

---

[20] A. W. Tozer, *The Divine Conquest*, Fleming H. Revell Co., pp. 127, 128.
[21] A. W. Tozer, *The Pursuit of God*, Christian Publications Inc., pp. 58, 59.

aim before you: to be "well-pleasing to Him." It's a new way of living. You've taken another person into your life. Let your life revolve around Him; study how to please Him. Consider His tastes, His likes and dislikes. Allow nothing distasteful to Him. Life for you will become sweet and satisfying.[22]

These quotations demonstrate essential agreement as to the nature and simplicity of the deeper Christian life. The authors have used their own style and illustrations and have often based their statements on different passages of Scripture; but they are unanimous in concluding that real spirituality is the result of a continuous conscious fellowship with Christ by the power of the Spirit. To habitually count on the presence and power of the Lord is the secret of abundant Christian living.

It is important to note that walking with the Lord brings every realm and detail of life into the orbit of the spiritual. This aspect of the truth has been well stated by J. Gregory Mantle:

Many Christians have yet to learn the meaning of that word, "Whether therefore ye eat or drink, or whatsoever ye do, do all to the glory of God," for to take step by step by the Spirit means that our meat and drink, and everything that touches the domain of our senses, must ever be placed under a sacred discipline. The same discipline is equally indispensable for the life of our affections and thoughts; for our reading, for our recreation, for our literary and artistic pursuits. To

---

[22] Norman B. Harrison, *New Testament Living*, The Harrison Service, pp. 53, 54.

ignore the guidance of the Holy Spirit in any one of these departments of life is to cause Him grief, and to forfeit the spiritual power of which He would have us to be the unfailing aqueducts to a dying world. . . . The two realms, which men have designated secular and sacred, will "melt into each other as the roseate streaks of dawn melt into the splendors of the morning" as we take step by step by the Spirit, for when the Spirit of Christ breathes through our life the meanest occupation becomes divine. Nothing is little or great with regard to the things of God. Everything that bears the impress of His will is great, however trifling it may appear. It is this alone which gives value to the duties of our life, and nothing can be regarded as small or insignificant that is the object of His desire. A natural tendency to untidiness is easily overcome if, for His sake, and that we may please Him in everything, we keep the room or the papers in order.[23]

The heart that is thirsty for God may be helped by some suggestions as to the conditions or condition of entering the abiding life in Christ. Professor Steven Barabas discusses this problem in his book, *So Great Salvation*, which gives the history and doctrine of the Keswick movement. He points out that, though authorities differ on the number of conditions or steps deemed necessary to experience the abundant life, all the conditions may be reduced to one:

---

[23] J. Gregory Mantle, *Beyond Humiliation*, Used by permission of the Moody Bible Institute, Moody Press, 820 N. LaSalle Street, Chicago 10, Illinois, pp. 233, 235.

G. Campbell Morgan suggests only two conditions for the filling of the Spirit—abandonment and abiding. The blessing is first realized by the abandonment; it is maintained by abiding. By "abandonment," Dr. Morgan means handing over to the control of God the whole life, in order that through that life His will may be realized and His work done. The life thus abandoned to God is a life that has given up its own plans, purposes, and hopes; and has taken instead the plan, the purpose, and the hope of God. By "abiding" he means continuing to live a life of abandonment; regarding Christ as Lord always, entering into no transaction of business or of pleasure without taking Him into account, treating Him as the ever-present King by saying to Him at all seasons and hours and everywhere, "Master, is this Thy will?" "If men are filled with the Spirit by abandonment, they continue filled with the Spirit by abiding." . . . It will be observed that although various suggestions are made above as a guide to those who desire the fullness of the Spirit no hard-and-fast rules are set forth as the only condition of the fullness. The suggestions made are scriptural ones in every case. Although they differ in number—Andrew Murray, for example, offering seven, and G. Campbell Morgan only two—and although they are worded differently, they are essentially the same, and may be reduced to only one: the fullness of the spirit may become the believer's experience if in all things he recognizes the sovereignty and the lordship of Christ in his life, and if he allows the Holy Spirit to become his Teacher, his Guide, his Power for sanctification and service. To be filled by the Spirit means to be controlled by the Spirit. Evan Hopkins used often to say that instead of seeking to have more of the Holy Spirit, we should yield ourselves to Him, that He might have more of us.[24]

The unknown author of *How to Live the Victorious Christian Life*, calls "surrender" the one condition of attaining such a life, and appeals to the experience of Brother Lawrence:

> How can we get this indwelling of Christ? And how know we have Him and thus "know Him and the power of His Resurrection"? How did Brother Lawrence get his blessing? How did he keep it? He just surrendered himself entirely to God. Without such surrender one cannot really practice the presence of God. "I know," said he, "that for the right practice of it, the heart must be empty of all other things; because God will possess the heart ALONE. And as He cannot possess it alone without emptying it of all beside, so neither can He act there and do in it what he pleases unless it be left vacant to Him. . . ." When he possesses us wholly, then we shall be holy. Are we willing to take the step? Are we willing to put ourselves unreservedly into His hands? To do so is to secure heaven on earth![25]

It is doubtless true that surrender is the indispensable and all inclusive condition of entering the life of constant fellowship with God. However, the blessed experience of communion with the Lord deserves greater emphasis than the condition upon which it rests. Therefore, it seems better to describe the condition of this higher life as simply "abiding" or "walking with the Lord."

---

[24] Steven Barabas, *So Great Salvation*, Fleming H. Revell Co., pp. 144, 145.
[25] Unknown Author, *How To Live the Victorious Christian Life*, Zondervan Publishing House, pp. 39, 40.

It should be understood that this new life does not mean sinless perfection or the loss of the tendency to sin. Evan Hopkins, one of the fathers of the Keswick movement, has given a helpful word on this point:

> But there are some who seem to think we may be freed in this life from all tendency to sin. There are some who seem to maintain that the blessing of being "pure in heart" is a state of purity, rather than a maintained condition of purity. This distinction is important. . . . It may be made clear by an illustration. Let us suppose a natural impossibility; namely, that by passing a lighted candle through a dark room such an effect is produced by that one act, that the room not only becomes instantly lighted, but continues in a state of illumination. If this were possible, the room would not be dependent on the continued presence of the lighted candle for its light, though it would be indebted to the candle in the first instance for the state of light introduced to it. . . . Such is not, we maintain, the nature of the cleansing which Christ bestows upon us. . . . Adopting the same illustration—but without supposing an impossibility—let the darkness represent sin, and the light holiness. What the lighted candle is to the dark room, Christ is to the heart of the believer. . . . By the light of His own indwelling presence He keeps sin outside the region of our consciousness. The cleansing thus brought about and realized is not a state, but a maintained condition, having no existence whatever apart from Christ Himself.[26]

---

[26] Evan Hopkins, op. cit., pp. 25, 26.

This clear instruction about the life of holiness being a maintained condition and not a state is most important. It helps us to understand why we succeed and why we so often fail. We fail because we leave the light of His presence. We succeed by "walking in the light," which is nothing else but walking with the Lord. This is the message of I John 1:5-7.

> And this is the message—the message of promise—which we have heard from Him and now are reporting to you: God is Light and there is no darkness in Him at all—no, not in any way. . . . (So) if we say we are partakers together and enjoy fellowship with Him when we live and move and are walking about in darkness, we are (both) speaking falsely and do not live and practice the Truth (of the Gospel) . . . But if we (really) are living and walking in the Light as He (Himself) is in the Light, we have (true, unbroken) fellowship with one another, and the blood of Jesus Christ His Son cleanses (removes) us from all sin and guilt—keeps us cleansed from sin in all its forms and manifestations. (The Amplified New Testament)

The victory that comes by walking with the Lord is thus His accomplishment and leaves no room for boasting. He is our holiness.

But if the condition of this better life is so simple, why do most of us come so far short in our experience? Perhaps because our "pursuit of God" is not sufficiently persistent. We are too easily discouraged by our failures. Perhaps also because we tend to depend more on feeling than on faith.

Faith takes God at His word in spite of inner experience or circumstances. Here the helpful counsel of Orson R. Palmer should be read and reread:

> God's own fullness in our lives may not transport us from the valley to the mountain top; it may not be a mighty tide of feeling, which surges over our souls. On the contrary it may seem a long time coming. Learn to hold fast your confidence to the end. He is faithful who promised and will not disappoint those who trust in Him (Heb. 10:23). Through the tears, the struggles, the failures, the disappointments, the darkness, "stand fast in the Lord," abide in Christ. You came to Him as a poor, undone sinner and found Him precious as a Saviour. The experiences you have been passing through were your school in which you learned of Christ, and in Him you found rest. All you need has been wrought out for you at the cross; and the Holy Spirit will make it real within you if you will but quietly and patiently ABIDE IN CHRIST. Say with each day, in its trials and perplexities, its shadow or sunshine: I will abide. I do abide in Him. He will abide in you. Trust Him to live out His life, to perfect His work, to pray His prayers, to travail for others, to intercede, to work in and through you. There can be no failure if the government be on His shoulders, and of the increase of it there shall be no end; God's purposes in and through your life may be wrought out slowly. So He works in nature. The tree, flower, and the plant do not grow in a day.[27]

---

[27] Orson R. Palmer, *Deliverance From the Penalty and Power of Sin*, Moody Press, pp. 104, 105.

Walking with the Lord does take perseverance and constant practice. The following suggestions should prove helpful:

> Realize His presence within you, and without you. Use your imagination to realize that He is always present. Practice realizing His presence constantly. This is what is meant by "pray without ceasing." . . . Your senses cannot find Him, but if you think of Him constantly, His presence will become more and more real to you.[28]

The experience of F. B. Meyer as related by Stanley Frodsham shows how the power of the Lord may be counted on for victory over the temptations to impatience and irritability that beset us each day:

> F. B. Meyer tells of a simple incident that revolutionized his whole life. He had been having a day of fellowship with some ministerial brethren. They had been talking of the life of giving up all for Christ; when one minister remarked that his life had become one of "intaking from Christ." He told of being with some children who were very inattentive and restless, but when he was tempted to be impatient he looked up into the face of the Lord and said, "Thy patience, Lord!" Instantly the Lord dropped into his heart His own patience. He testified, "I have always dared to believe that God put me into difficult situations to reveal things in Christ which I was to claim. In a moment when I am tempted to irritability, I say, "Thy sweetness; Lord." In a moment of weakness,

[28] Alice Bishop Kramer and Albert Ludlow Kramer, *The Life in the Vine*, Fleming H. Revell Co., p. 18.

"Thy strength, Lord." Meyer that night learned the secret of in-taking, a lesson that he never forgot. You will find in Christ all you need for every occasion. You will have temptations but look away from yourself to Him who is your Saviour, continually express to Him your greatest need, "Thy Spirit, Lord!" and He will not fail to give.[29]

It will be found that great blessing will attend the giving of special attention to realizing the presence of the Lord at the times of going to sleep at night and awaking in the morning. The following testimony of Dr. Barnhouse shows how such exercise makes "the outgoings of the morning and evening to rejoice" (Ps. 65:8b):

> I frequently noticed that I awoke in the morning thinking the same thoughts that had been in my mind at the time I closed my eyes in sleep the night before. Many people know from sad experience that the mind frequently drifts to thoughts that are utterly of self, and its interests and desires, in those half-awake moments that end our day and that begin our night. I discovered, therefore, that it was of great importance to capture this half-world of the mind for our Lord Jesus Christ . . . . One morning when I awoke trying to solve a chess problem that had filled my mind as I had put my head upon my pillow, I became conscious of this law and determined that, henceforth, I would go to sleep thinking of Christ. As the months passed, I discovered that there was much more than a habit involved in this. Here was a proof of the presence of

[29] Stanley Fordsham, <i>The Spirit Filled Life</i>, Wm. B. Eerdmans Publishing Co., p. 27.

the Lord Jesus Christ in my heart and mind, controlling even the subconscious element of my life. Then I learned that I must not merely go to sleep thinking about Christ but that I must go to sleep in communion with Him. I began memorizing verses of Scripture at night and reciting them as I fell asleep. Soon He became more real than the inside of my eyelids. I could not see them though they were close to my eyes; Him I learned to know in everything but the touch. And closing one's eyes with Christ takes away all fear of sleepless nights. Let others count sheep jumping over a wall; I shall talk with the Shepherd. "He giveth His beloved sleep" (Ps. 127:2). "I laid me down and slept," says David, "I awaked; for the Lord sustained me" (Ps. 3:5).

> When sleep her balm denies
> My silent spirit sighs,
>> May Jesus Christ be praised!
> The night becomes as day
> When from the heart we say
>> May Jesus Christ be praised!

Then when I awake to a new day, I wake to hear Him speak to me, and I to Him. David knew this when he said; "When I awake, I am still with thee" (Ps. 139:18).[30]

The life under grace can be a continuous experience of glorious fellowship with the Son of God. It is a miracle life which, like the miracle of creation, is made possible in our dark hearts only by the supernatural light from the face of Christ: "For God, who commanded the light to shine out

---

[30] Donald Grey Barnhouse, *God's Methods for Holy Living.* Eternity Book Service, pp. 85, 86.

of darkness, hath shined in our hearts, to give the light of the knowledge of the glory of God in the face of Jesus Christ" (2 Cor. 4:6).

This allegory of Mark Guy Pearce is a beautiful summary of all that has been quoted and said about the way of life under grace:

I wondered within myself where Holiness dwelt, but I feared to go in search for her. I knew she would never be at home in the lowlands and busy streets of Mansoul. All whom I asked about her, answered doubtfully. One said that she had died long ago; indeed was buried in Eden before Adam came out. One said that she lived away at the end of the Valley of the Shadow of Death, her house was on the brink of the river, and that I must hope to meet with her just before I crossed it. Another argued almost angrily against the notion. "Nay," said he, "she lives farther on still; search as thou wilt, thou shalt never find her till thou art landed on the shores of the Celestial City." . . . Then I remembered how well I had fared aforetime on the Holy Hill, and went forth again. So up the lonely way I went, and reached the top of it and looked once more upon my blessed Saviour. And lo! there was Holiness sitting at the Master's feet. I feared to say that I had been looking for her, but as I gazed upon the Crucified, and felt the greatness of His love to me, and as all my heart went out in love and adoration, Holiness rose up, and came to me all graciously, and said: "I have been waiting for thee ever since thy first coming." "Waiting there?" I asked wondering. "At His feet," said Holiness; "I am always there."[31]

---

[31] *Deeper Experiences of Famous Christians*, Pilgrim Tract Society, Randleman, N. C.

Chapter 2

CONFUSION OF LAW AND GRACE

"The Christian world has never very clearly perceived what was its relation to the Old Testament religion. How discordant and inconsistent have been the prevailing views on this subject."[1] The following quotations will show the accuracy of this observation made by the one-time professor of systematic theology at Yale University:

> "The law is a rule of life for believers, reminding them of their duties and leading them in the way of life and salvation."[2]

> "The moral precepts are not repealed. The entire deca-logue is brought into the Christian code by a distinct injunction of its separate parts."[3]

---

[1] George Barker Stevens, *The Theology of the New Testament*, Charles Scribner's Sons, p. 23.
[2] L. Berkhof, *Systematic Theology*, Wm. B. Eerdmans Publishing Co., p. 615.
[3] Richard Watson, *Theological Institutes*, II, Carlton and Phillips Publishing Co., p. 471.

"Grace has in no sense superseded law." "Obedience to law puts one in the midstream of God's purpose."[4]

"Christ does not free us from the law as a rule of life."[5]

"Christians should recite the commandments (as their creeds) to keep in memory what they must do to enter into life."[6]

"The law is a declaration of the will of God for man's salvation." "The clearest illustration of the desire of Dispensationalists to eliminate everything that savours of obedience from the dispensation of promise and of grace and to confine it to the dispensation of law, is found in their insistence that the Decalogue is not intended for the Church. . . . The Ten Commandments are an important part of all the great Protestant catechisms. But Dispensationalists insist that they are not intended for this dispensation."[7]

"Genuine sanctification will show itself in habitual respect to God's law, and habitual effort to live in obedience to it as the rule of life. There is no greater mistake than to suppose that a Christian has nothing to do with the law and the Ten Commandments, because he cannot be justified by keeping them."[8]

---

[4] P. B. Fitzwater, *Systematic Theology*, Wm. B. Eerdmans Publishing Co., pp. 9, 359.
[5] A. Strong, *Systematic Theology*, The Judson Press, p. 876.
[6] William B. Pope, *A Compendium of Christian Theology*, III, Phillips & Hunt, p. 174.
[7] Oswald T. Allis, *Prophecy and the Church*, The Presbyterian and Reformed Publishing Co., pp. 39, 46-47.
[8] J. C. Ryle, *Holiness*, Fleming H. Revell Co., p. 27.

"If, therefore, it is heresy for a Christian to boast that he is experimentally 'dead indeed unto sin,' it must be no less a heresy to boast that one is actually 'not under law' as a rule of conduct for his life. For what is sin if it be not the transgression of law."[9]

"Should it be said that it is only exemption from obligation to the moral law or ten commandments that is pleaded for, and not the law or will of God in general, I answer, the ten commandments are the summary or synopsis of God's will as to the regulation of man's life; and every other part of the Bible is in harmony with this law. So, that exemption from compliance with any Bible statute, or from the obligation of submitting ourselves to any Bible truth, might be pleaded for as properly as exemption from the law. For the law cannot be cut out of the Bible and set aside by itself, while all else remains in force. Either all must go or none."[10]

"I should reckon it next to impossible for any one of unbiased mind—with no peculiar theory to support—with no desire of any kind, but that of giving a fair and natural interpretation to the teaching of Scriptures—to weigh calmly the series of statements now adduced, and to derive from them any other impression than this—that the moral law, as revealed in the Old Testament, had with the apostles of our Lord a recognized place in the Christian church, and was plainly set forth by them as the grand test of excellence, and the authoritative rule of life. They recognized and appealed to it thus simply as

---

[9] L. E. Maxwell, *Crowded to Christ*, Wm. B. Eerdmans Publishing Co., p. 222.
[10] Horatius Bonar, *God's Way of Holiness*, Moody Press, p. 72.

it stood in the written revelation of God, and because so written,—knowing nothing, apparently, of the refined explanations of modern thought, which would hold the morality of the law, indeed, to be binding on Christians, but not as commanded in the law—that while the substance or principles of the law may be said to be still living, in its outward and commanding form it is dead—or that, as formally expressed law, it is no longer obligatory, whether with reference to justification, or as a rule of life."[11]

"The liberty we enjoy as Christians is not a licentious liberty: Though Christ has redeemed us from the curse of the law he has not freed us from the obligation of it."[12]

This list of quotations could be extended indefinitely but these are sufficient to show the typical positions regarding the law of the Old Testament. Doubtless all would agree that there is some sense in which the New Testament believer is not under the law of Moses, but it is equally clear that all agree that there is some sense in which the Mosaic law is still binding upon the Christian. Our problem is to discover whether the New Testament teaches any degree of obligation to the Mosaic system.

---

[11] Patrick Fairbairn, *The Revelation of Law in Scripture*, Zondervan Publishing House, p. 274.

[12] *Matthew Henry's Commentary*, Fleming H. Revell Co., VI, p. 675.

Chapter 3

PRIMARY CAUSES OF CONFUSION

One of the principal causes of misunderstanding about law and grace is the failure to define terms. The word *law* (*nomos*) has several meanings in the Bible. Robert Mc-Quilkin has listed the following twelve different uses of the word *law* in the New Testament: (1) The Pentateuch (Lk. 24:44); (2) The Old Testament (Jn. 12:34; 15:25); (3) The Mosaic Law; (4) The Ten Commandments (Ex. 20); (5) The Moral Law (Mt. 22:37-40); (6) Some particular Precept or Regulation of the Law (Jn. 19:7); (7) The Ceremonial Law (Heb. 7:28; 8:4; 9:22); (8) Law as Principle (Rom. 3:37; 8:2); (9) Law in General (Rom. 7:1, 2); (10) Law as Penalty (Rom. 4:15; Gal. 3:10; (11) Law as Contrasted with Grace (Gal. 3:11; Mt. 23:23); (12) The Law of Christ (Gal. 6:2; James 1:25; 2:12). Concerning moral law, McQuilkin correctly observes: "The moral law is not equivalent to the Mosaic Law. However, the Mosaic law, which was 'added' because of transgressions, included the moral law. It included also the ceremonial law, civil law, criminal law, sanitary law, governmental law. But the moral law existed before Moses, and continues after the Cross."[1]

Doubtless some of these uses of the term "law" are only aspects of the Mosaic law and could be combined. However, the analysis is helpful in emphasizing the importance of defining terms in this area of doctrine.

Lewis Sperry Chafer lists six subdivisions of the Bible doctrine of law as follows: (1) Natural, inherent, or intrinsic (Lev. 11:44; I Peter 1:16); (2) Prescribed by man (Luke 20:22; Acts 19:38); (3) Law of Moses (Ex. 20 f.); (4) Revealed will of God in any form (Rom. 7:15-25); (5) Messianic rule of life for the kingdom (Mt. 5:1-7:29); (6) Law of Christ (I Cor. 9:20-21; Gal. 6:2).[2]

What Chafer calls natural, inherent, or intrinsic law is called the moral law by McQuilkin. For the sake of simplicity we shall use the term moral law to describe the eternal principles of righteousness which are a reflection of the character of God. This law has always existed and is the essence of the will of God for every dispensation. Its standards are as high as the glory or character of God (Rom. 3:23), and its obligations rest alike upon all created intelligences.

Much of the confusion over law and grace is caused by the failure to distinguish the moral law from the Mosaic law—especially from the Ten Commandments. When so many commentators and theologians say that the Ten Commandments have never been repealed or abrogated

---

[1] Robert McQuilkin, *Law and Grace*, Wm. B. Eerdmans Publishing Co., p. 9 f.
[2] Lewis Sperry Chafer, *Systematic Theology*, Dallas Seminary Press, VII, p. 225-26.

they really mean that the moral law of God is eternal. This conclusion no one would question. But the moral law of God is not identical with the Mosaic Ten Commandments. Laws based upon the same moral principle are not necessarily identical. The law of Michigan against homicide is not the same as the law of Illinois for the same offense, although both are based on the same moral principle. In Illinois capital punishment may be imposed for first degree murder while in Michigan capital punishment is illegal.

The penalty for certain violations of each of the Mosaic Ten Commandments was death. No nation or church can honestly claim to be under the Mosaic Ten Commandments. But all people in every dispensation are under the moral law of God. Moses did not originate this law and it did not cease with the cross.

To avoid confusion and legalism a careful distinction should be made between the moral law and the Mosaic Ten Commandments. When so many say that the Ten Commandments apply to Christians as fully as they ever did to Israel they mean that the moral principles of the law are still binding. But this is not what they have expressed. If the Ten Commandments of the law are still binding then all of the penalties must remain the same. The death penalties should be imposed for Sabbath-breaking, idolatry, adultery, rebellion against parents, etc. To change the penalty of a law means to abolish that law. A law without a penalty is an anomaly. A law with its penalty abolished is only good advice. That all of this is not pointless hairsplitting is as evident as the difference between life and death. It is just this difference that is indicated by Paul's description of the Ten Commandments as "the ministration of death, written and engraven in stones" (2 Cor. 3:7a).

Horatius Bonar is often quoted with approval by those who maintain that the believer of this age is yet in some sense under the law of Moses. Bonar's confusing discussion of "The Saint and the Law,"[3] is tinged with legalism because of his failure to distinguish the moral law from the Mosaic law. This sample quotation is typical: "Yes, Christ 'hath redeemed us from the curse of the law,' but certainly not from the law itself; for that would be to redeem us from a divine rule and guide; it would be to redeem us from that which is 'holy, just, and good.'"[4] To thus identify the moral law with the Mosaic is to be involved in serious legalism. Bonar overlooks the fact that the same New Testament book which declares the believer is redeemed from the curse of the law also teaches that he is redeemed from the law itself: "To redeem them that were under the law, that we might receive the adoption of sons" (Gal. 4:5). The temporary institution of the Mosaic economy embodied the moral law but did not initiate it, and certainly the termination of the Mosaic law did not terminate the moral law.

Consider another example. When A. Strong writes, "Christ does not free us from the law as a rule of life,"[5] he evidently means that the Christian is under the same moral law as that which is embodied in the Mosaic law. However, he has fallen into the common error of identifying the Mosaic with the moral law. The New

---

[3] Bonar, op. cit., Ch. VI.

[4] Ibid., p. 74.

[5] Strong, loc. cit.

Testament is just as emphatic that the believer is not under the law for sanctification as it is that he is not under the law for justification: "For sin shall not have dominion over you: for ye are not under the law, but under grace" (Rom. 6:14). "But if ye be led of the Spirit, ye are not under the law" (Gal. 5:18).

Fairbairn's book, *The Revelation of Law in Scripture*, has long been considered a classic in its field, but even Fairbairn becomes inconsistent when he deals with the Christian's relation to the Mosaic law:

> I should reckon it next to impossible for any one of unbiased mind—with no peculiar theory to support—with no desire of any kind, but that of giving a fair and natural interpretation to the teaching of Scripture—to weight calmly the series of statements now adduced, and to derive from them any other impression than this—that the moral law, as revealed in the Old Testament, had with the apostles of our Lord a recognized place in the Christian church, and was plainly set forth by them as the grand test of excellence, and the authoritative rule of life. They recognized and appealed to it thus simply as it stood in the written revelation of God, and because so written;—knowing nothing, apparently, of the refined explanations of modern thought, which would hold the morality of the law, indeed, to be binding on Christians, but not as commanded in the law—that while the substance or principles of the law may he said to be still living, in its outward and commanding form it is dead—or that, as formally expressed law, it is no longer obligatory, whether with reference to justification, or as a rule of life. And yet, unquestionably, there is

something in the apostolic mode of contemplating the law which gives a certain color to these representations. A marked distinction is made in various places between the position which Israel occupied toward the law, and that now occupied by believers in Christ; such, that there is a sense in which Israel was placed under it, and in which Christians are not; that it had a purpose to serve till the fulfilment of the covenant of promise in Christ, for which it is no longer specifically required; that somehow it is done away or abolished, or, as it is again put, that we are done away from it, that is set free, in regard to its right to lord it over us; that we are even dead to it, or are no longer under it; and that the scope or end for which the law was given is accomplished, and alone can be accomplished, in Christ for those who are spiritually united to Him (2 Cor. 3:11; Eph. 2:15; Col. 2:14; Rom. 6:14; 7:4; Gal. 3:19-25, 4:1-6; Rom. 7:6; Rom. 8:3, 4, 10:4).[6]

In the first part of this quotation Fairbairn places the Christian under the law as written in the Old Testament for his rule of life. But then he proceeds to modify this conclusion by the admission that "somehow" the New Testament "gives a certain color" to the representations of his opponents that the law is done away or abolished. How laws can be abolished and still remain binding as written he fails to explain clearly. His attempted resolution of the paradox is that we are "delivered from it (the law), only that we may be brought into conformity to its spirit

---

[6] Fairbairn, op. cit., pp. 274-275.

and requirements."[7] All of this yes-and-no attitude toward the law can be avoided by a simple distinction between the eternal moral law of God and the Mosaic law. The first is as immutable as the character of God but the second was temporary and has been abolished.

Even Robert McQuilkin, who first gives the careful distinction between the moral law and the Mosaic law, seems to forget that distinction later when he writes:

> "All of the references in the New Testament, direct or indirect to the ten commandments would suggest that it is taken for granted that the ten commandments apply to Christians as fully as they ever did to Israel."[8]

If all of the other quotations given in chapter two are noted carefully, it will be discovered that in each case the apparent legalism is caused by a failure to distinguish between the eternal moral law of God and the Mosaic legal system. To avoid any and every degree of legalism this distinction is absolutely vital and necessary.

---

[7] Ibid., p. 279.
[8] McQuilkin, op. cit., p. 41.

Chapter 4

THE LAW OF MOSES A UNIT

It is common to divide the Mosaic law into three parts: the Ten Commandments (often called the moral law), the ordinances, and the judgments. The ordinances are the laws governing Israel's religious life while the judgments are the civil laws. These divisions are sometimes helpful for analysis and study but actually have no Scriptural authority. Many of Israel's laws would belong in two of the suggested divisions. For example, the law of the tithe is both religious and civil. The Ten Commandments have a prominent place in the law but Christ taught that the greatest commandment was not one of the ten (Mt. 22:36-37).

As a matter of fact both the Old and New Testaments regard the law of Moses as an indivisible unit (Jas. 2:10; Gal. 5:3; Josh. 1:8).

In Ephesians 6:1-2 Paul refers to the fifth commandment and comments that it "is the first commandment with promise." In fact it is the only one of the Ten Commandments which has an accompanying promise. This means that Paul's use of the word commandment embraces the other laws outside of the ten. The problem of whether or not Paul's reference here places the Christian under the Ten Commandments will be dealt with later. Now we are concerned only with the bearing of this passage on the unity of the law of Moses.

In Galatians 3:17 Paul speaks of "the law" which was given four hundred and thirty years after the promise to Abraham. It should be evident that in this passage and context "the law" means the entire Mosaic legislation as given at Mount Sinai, and cannot refer only to the ceremonial laws—as some maintain. It should also be apparent that by "the law" Paul does not mean the man-made laws and traditions which were later added to the law of Moses. There were no such man-made laws when the law was first given in its purity. Yet some writers maintain that the Galatian polemic against "the law" is to be understood as only directed against the man-made laws and traditions of the Jews. Such an interpretation is further embarrassed by Galatians 3:10: "For as many as are of the works of the law are under the curse: for it is written, Cursed is every one that continueth not in all things which are written in the book of the law, to do them." Here Paul identifies "the law" about which he is speaking by quoting part of it from the Book of Deuteronomy.

According to orthodox Jewish tradition, there are 613 commandments in the law of Moses. These are divided into 248 affirmative laws and 365 negative laws. Moses Margoliouth, who was one of the translators of the English Revised Version, published a catalog of the

613 commandments in English in 1743. In this list the Ten Commandments are not placed first and there is no indication of special emphasis or importance above the others. In fact, the usual Ten Commandments are expanded into thirteen laws. This is done by dividing Exodus 20:4-5 into three separate injunctions against idolatry and making two laws out of the fourth commandment concerning the Sabbath. These thirteen laws are serially numbered from twenty-six to thirty-eight in the long list of 613 laws. There is no attempt to separate or classify different kinds of laws. The listing is on the basis of the order of the occurrence of the laws from Genesis through Deuteronomy. All of this shows that orthodox Judaism believes the Mosaic laws constitute a unified system and that all the laws are equally binding.

Outstanding commentators concur in the opinion that the Mosaic law is a unit. Meyer says: "In *nomos* (law), however, to think merely of the moral law is erroneous; and the distinction between the ritualistic, civil, and moral law is modern."[1]

Stevens observes: "It is common to make a distinction between the ceremonial and the moral parts of the law, and to suppose that, while the former are done away, the latter are still binding upon Christians. But this distinction is recognized neither in the Old Testament nor in the New; it is a modern division of the law which is quite convenient and natural for us to make, but one of which a quite unwarrantable use is commonly made."[2]

---

[1] Heinrich A. W. Meyer, *Commentary on the New Testament*, I, Funk and Wagnalls Co., p. 120.

[2] Stevens, op. cit., footnote, p. 24.

With this Godet agrees: "In general, the distinction between the ritual and moral elements of the law is foreign to the Jewish conscience, which takes the law as a divine unity."[3]

James Denny points out that, with one exception, in a quotation from Jeremiah 31:33 in Hebrews 8:10 and 10:16, the word *law* is always singular in the New Testament. This points to the unity of the divine laws.

W. R. Nicoll declares: "This distinction between the moral and ceremonial law has no meaning in Paul."[4]

"Thus with the introduction of the present period of salvation there remain the general moral principles ruling the realm of the earlier period (Rom. 6:4; 13:8-10), even though in a completely new spirit; for the law is a unity (Jas. 2:10), and as such is wholly abolished."[5]

The following passage is often cited to show that only the ordinances of the law were abolished at the cross:

> Having blotted out the bond written in ordinances that was against us, which was contrary to us; and he hath taken it out of the way, nailing it to the cross; having despoiled the principalities and powers, he made a show of them openly, triumphing over them in it. Let no man therefore judge you in meat, or in drink, or in respect of a least day or a new moon or a sabbath day: which are a shadow of the things to come; but the body is Christ's (Col. 2:14-17, ASV).

---

[3] F. Godet, *Commentary on Romans*, T. & T. Clark Publishing Co., p. 144.

[4] W. Robertson Nicoll, *The Expositor's Greek Testament*, Wm. B. Eerdmans Publishing Co., III, p. 527.

[5] Erich Sauer, *The Dawn of World Redemption*, Wm. B. Eerdmans Publishing Co., p. 194.

But here the term *ordinances* is used in a general sense to describe all of the Mosaic laws. The idea that only ceremonial laws are involved is cancelled by the reference to "a sabbath day" in verse sixteen. Even Patrick Fairbairn, who thinks there is a sense in which the Mosaic law is not abolished, acknowledges that the whole law is intended by this passage. In commenting on Colossians 2:14-17 he says: "This, there can be no doubt, was the law, not in part but in whole—the law in the full compass of its requirements . . ."[6]

Thus orthodox Jewish tradition, able commentators, and the Scriptures themselves recognize that the law of Moses is an indivisible unit. This presents an insurmountable problem for any degree of Mosaic legalism. No modern legalist wants to climb to the top of Mount Sinai with its fire and thunder but many think it is a good thing to take a short hike up its foothills. But to touch the mountain at the bottom was as fatal as climbing to the top (Heb. 12:18-21). The unity of the Mosaic law leaves only two alternatives— either complete deliverance from, or complete subjection to the entire system. It will be shown that the first of these alternatives is clearly taught in the New Testament.

---

[6] Fairbairn, op. cit., p. 466.

Chapter 5

THE MOSAIC LAW DONE AWAY

The Mosaic law was of the nature of a covenant made with Israel alone. "Thus shalt thou say to the house of Jacob, and tell the children of Israel . . . Now therefore, if ye will obey my voice indeed, and keep my covenant, then ye shall be a peculiar treasure unto me above all people: for all the earth is mine" (Ex. 19:3b, 5). This covenant in no sense superseded or canceled the earlier Abrahamic covenant of promise (Gal. 3:14-18). It was added as a temporary institution until Christ should come. "Wherefore then serveth the law? It was added because of transgression, till the seed should come to whom the promise was made; and it was ordained by angels in the hand of a mediator" (Gal. 3:19).

It needs to be emphasized that the end of the Mosaic law, including the Ten Commandments, does not cancel or detract one iota from the eternal moral law of God. The moral principles of the ten laws did not begin with Sinai but are as eternal and immutable as the character of God. To understand this should dispel the fears of those who think the abolition of the Mosaic law leaves only a state of lawlessness.

The moral principles embodied in the law of Moses Paul calls "the righteousness of the law" (Rom. 8:4), and shows that such principles are the goal of the Spirit-directed life in the same context in which he teaches the believer is not under the Mosaic law (Rom. 6-8).

This should be no more difficult to understand than the fact that a citizen of the United States is not under the laws of Canada, even though the moral principles underlying the laws of the two countries are the same. When a citizen of the United States becomes a citizen of Canada he does not remain under ten of the best laws of the United States. Nor does the fact that some of the laws of the United States are quite similar to some of the laws of Canada confuse or compromise his new exclusive responsibility to Canada. So the believing Jew of the first century moved entirely from the Mosaic economy of law into the new economy of grace instituted by Jesus Christ (John 1:17).

Both Hebrews and Galatians were written to prove that the entire Mosaic system has been abolished and superseded by the better things of the grace of Christ. Whole chapters and large sections of other epistles are devoted to the same theme. The large proportion of the New Testament written to teach freedom from the law is doubtless a divine provision to guard against the persistent and widespread legalism of every generation. Since there is so much Scripture teaching freedom from the law, we shall confine our attention to several passages which show clearly that the entire Mosaic system—including the Ten Commandments—is done away.

In Galatians 3:17 Paul identifies the law about which he is talking as that which was given four hundred and thirty years after the promise to Abraham. This dating of the beginning of the law shows that he is speaking of the entire Mosaic system given at Mount Sinai, and not just part of the law. Further in the same context Paul declares: "So that the law is become our tutor to bring us unto Christ, that we might be justified by faith. But now that faith is come, we are no longer under a tutor" (Gal. 3:24-25, ASV). Since the law is described as a temporary tutor until Christ, the conclusion is definite that now that Christ has come the authority of the tutor has ceased.

In Romans 7:4 Paul declares that the believer is "dead to the law by the body of Christ." Continuing his argument he says, "but now we are delivered from the law, that being dead wherein we were held; that we should serve in newness of spirit, and not in the oldness of the letter. What shall we say then? Is the law sin? God forbid. Nay, I had not known sin, but by the law; for I had not known lust, except the law had said, Thou shalt not covet" (Rom. 7:6-7). This passage shows that the law, from which we are delivered, includes the Ten Commandments, for Paul specifically quotes the tenth commandment as part of the law of which he speaks.

But there are those who say that deliverance from the law does not mean that the law is abolished or abrogated. Then what else can be meant by the language of 2 Corinthians 3:6-13?

Who also hath made us able ministers of the new testament; not of the letter, but of the spirit: for the letter killeth, but the spirit giveth life. But if the ministration of death, written and engraven in stones, was glorious, so that the children of Israel could not stedfastly behold the face of Moses for the glory of his countenance; which glory was to be done away: how shall not the ministration of the spirit be rather glorious? For if the ministration of condemnation be glory, much more doth the ministration of righteousness exceed in glory. For even that which was made glorious had no glory in this respect, by reason of the glory that excelleth. For if that which is done away was glorious, much more that which remaineth is glorious. Seeing then that we have such hope, we use great plainness of speech. And not as Moses, which put a vail over his face, that the children of Israel could not stedfastly look to the end of that which is abolished (2 Cor. 3:6-13).

In this passage the apostle is contrasting the new covenant with the old; the glory of Moses (as representative of the law) with the greater glory of grace; the bondage and condemnation of the law with the freedom and liberty of the Spirit. There can be no misunderstanding about the fact that the Mosaic system of this passage includes the Ten Commandments, because they are identified as "the ministration of death, written and engraven in stones" (2 Cor. 3:7a). Only the Ten Commandments were written in stones. However, Paul is talking about the entire Mosaic law as represented by its basic precepts. His description of the commandments as "the ministration of death" shows that he has in mind more than Exodus 20 because the death penalties for breaking the ten laws are found in other portions of the Pentateuch. But Paul's description also shows that these penalties are a vital part of the ten laws.

Three times in 2 Corinthians 3:6-13 it is declared that the Mosaic system is done away or abolished (vv. 7, 11, 13). The participle used in each of these three verses is from the verb *katargeo*, which means *to abrogate, to cancel, to bring to an end.* No stronger term could be found to describe the abolition of the law. It is the very word used to describe the destruction of the Antichrist in 2 Thessalonians 2:8.

In commenting on 2 Corinthians 3:7-13, L. S. Chafer says:

> It is the law as crystallized in the ten commandments which is in view; for that law alone was 'written and engraven in stones.' In the midst of the strongest possible contrast between the reign of the teachings of the law and the teachings of grace, it is declared that these commandments were 'done away' and 'abolished.' It should be recognized that the old was abolished to make place for the new, which far excels in glory. The passing of the law is not, therefore, a loss; it is rather an inestimable gain.[1]

In his discussion of the believer's relation to the law of God, Thiessen correctly observes:

> The Scriptures teach that in the death of Christ the believer is delivered, not only from the curse of the law (Gal. 3:10), that is, the penalty imposed upon him by the law, but from the law itself (Rom. 7:4; Eph. 2:14-

---

[1] Lewis Sperry Chafer, op. cit., Vol. IV, p. 242.

15; Col. 2:14, 20). It was at Calvary that Christ became the end of the law for righteousness (Rom. 10:4). That this includes the moral law as well as the ceremonial law is evident from 2 Corinthians 3:7-11. It is that which was 'written and engraven on stones,' that passed away. This surely refers to the ten commandments. As a result we are told that the believer is not 'under law, but under grace' (Rom. 6:14; 7:6; Gal. 4:30; 1:18), and he is exhorted to 'stand fast therefore, and be not entangled again in a yoke of bondage' (Gal. 5:1). From all of this it is very clear that Paul does not distinguish between the ceremonial and the moral law. He knows of only one law, and it is the law of God.[2]

Following many others, Thiessen uses the term *moral law* to describe the Ten Commandments. We prefer to use that expression in a different sense, to describe the eternal principles of righteousness which are a reflection of the character of God. However, if Thiessen's use of "moral law" is kept in mind, his discussion stands as an excellent summary of the Christian's relation to the law of Moses.

Alva J. McClain's answer to the question, "Is the Christian believer under the law?" should be read by every Bible student. The following brief extract from his answer is worth noting here:

The conclusion must be that the law itself as law, for the Christian, has been "abolished." No one can read the third chapter of II Corinthians with an unprejudiced attitude and not see that the writer is discussing the very

[2] Henry C. Thiessen, *Lectures in Systematic Theology*, Wm. B. Eerdmans Publishing Co., p. 241.

center of the law of God with its "tables of stone" (3). All this, so far as the Christian believer is concerned has been "done away" (11); it has been "abolished" (13).[3]

It is our opinion that one of the clearest and most profound discussions of the relation of the gospel to the law has been given by George Barker Stevens, one-time professor of Systematic Theology in Yale University in the days when Yale had not turned entirely to liberalism. The following quotation will also show that modern dispensationalists are not the first to have recognized a clear distinction between the law and grace:

> But when it is said the Old Testament system is abrogated in the new, it is of capital importance to observe that the new replaces the old, not by destruction, but by fulfillment. The new does not reject and discard the old; it preserves and embodies it, just so far as it has elements of permanent value for the world's religion. The fulfillment is therefore, an organic process; the new comes out of the old by a natural and orderly process of development. In that process what is essential and permanently useful is taken up into Christianity, more completely developed and applied, and reinforced by higher motives on the plane of broader principles.
>
> Christ did not fulfill a part of the law merely, but the whole of it. He did not complete the ritual part of the Old Testament alone, but all its moral parts as well. This is but to say that it was not merely the ritual element of the law which was imperfect and temporary, but the

---

[3] Alva J. McClain, *Law and the Christian Believer in Relation to the Doctrine of Grace*, Brethren Missionary Herald Co., Inc., p. 34.

moral element also. Many a moral maxim and practice of the Old Testament, as we have seen, was below the plane of Jesus' ideal morality. If he fulfills the system in all its parts, then must the system *as such* pass away. And this is the fact in the case. On no other supposition can the New Testament references to the subject be naturally explained; on no other view can a clear definition be given of the relation of the two Testaments.

The conclusion, then, to which we are led is, that the whole Old Testament system, in all its parts, was taken up into the process of fulfillment and that all its elements of permanent value and validity have been made part and parcel of the gospel. To the old system as such we have no need to go back, because the gospel is its completion, and we have no occasion to supplement Christianity by additions from Judaism. But the Old Testament has not thereby been *destroyed*, but *fulfilled*. On this distinction between destruction and fulfillment turns the true solution of the question under consideration. The fulfillment is, by its very nature, a conserving process; it rejects nothing which it can use, but embodies it in its perfect result. All the essentials of the Old Testament are preserved in the New, and it is as parts of the gospel of Christ that they are binding upon the Christian man. He is not under the Old Testament system, or, to state the case more fully, he is under only so much of it as has been taken up and incorporated into Christianity, and he is under that because it is a part of Christianity, not because it is a part of the Old Testament religion. If it is asked, Is not the Christian under the authority of the ten commandments? the reply is, In their Old Testament form and as part of that system, he is not. The essential substance of the ten commandments consists of changeless principles of righteousness, and is therefore a part of Christianity; in that sense the Christian is under the commandments, and in no other. The duty to obey parents, for example, is as urgently inculcated in the gospel as in the commandments, and is, of course, perpetually binding, but the reason by which it is enforced in the Old Testament—that by obedience one may win a long residence in the land of Canaan— is not applicable to us.

The truth which we are considering, stated on its positive side, is that Christianity is complete and sufficient in itself as a guide to faith and action. The whole philosophy of the subject is in that most expressive figure of Jesus to which we have referred: His gospel is not a patch to be sewed on the old garment of Judaism, but a wholly new garment.[4]

Such an excellent treatment stands without need of comment. The Christian is not under the Mosaic economy in any of its parts.

But in spite of all the evidence to support this conclusion many will still affirm that the Christian is under the Ten Commandments. They will ask, Should not a majority opinion be listened to on such an important matter? The next chapter will show why the Mosaic ten laws cannot apply to the Christian, but also that the New Testament believer is not without the highest moral obligations.

---

[4] Stevens, op. cit., pp. 23-25.

Chapter 6

THE NATURE OF THE MORAL LAW

When it is declared that all the Mosaic law, including the Ten Commandments, is done away, there is immediate opposition. Who dares to tamper with the Ten Commandments? It is constantly and emphatically affirmed that they have never been abrogated, canceled, or abolished.

It should be remembered that the Ten Commandments were part of the legal system of Israel as a theocracy. In this Mosaic economy "every transgression and disobedience received a just recompence of reward" (Heb. 2:2b). A law without a penalty is only good advice. The Mosaic penalty for violation of each of the first four commandments was death. For certain overt violations of all the other commandments the penalty was death. Only a theocracy could enforce such laws. No government, or denomination, or society even pretends to enforce them today. This is as it should be for they were given only to Israel and have long been abolished.

However, it is not only conceded but emphatically insisted that the moral principles of the ten laws are abiding and eternal. This is doubtless all that is meant by many who say these laws are still in force. But the moral law or the abiding principles of the Ten Commandments did not begin with Moses. The moral law is a reflection of the character of God and is as timeless as deity. All of the principles of the Ten Commandments not only reappear in the New Testament, but they appear in the Old Testament long before the Mosaic law was given. Cain's killing of Abel was murder even though it took place long before the Decalogue was written. All recognized that Jacob sinned when he stole Esau's blessing, even though the Mosaic eighth commandment had not been given. The moral law of God belongs to all ages and is written on the hearts of all men (Rom. 2:14-15). Carl Henry has correctly observed:

> The divine will was not for the first time disclosed in the Mosaic law (Gen. 2:16 ff., 8:15 ff., 9:1 ff.). Had there been no law from Adam to Moses, there would have been neither sin nor death (Rom. 5:12 ff.). To murder, to commit adultery, to steal, did not first become wrong with the proclamation of the Decalogue. Nor did it initially become wrong to steal and murder and covet when the Creator made known statutes and commandments to the original pair in the garden (Gen. 2:15). It had always been wrong to murder, to commit adultery, to steal, to covet. These are fundamental and universal principles that flow from the nature and will of God. Because the believer stands forever under the rule of God, he is obligated to God's moral demands. As the revelation of God's will, the moral law obliges the

Christian, granted that its Mosaic form is not primarily addressed to him. The eternal moral law is binding not on the believer in its Mosaic form, but the Old Testament moral law rather retains its force because it is a part of the righteous will of the immutable God?[1]

As would be expected, the infinitely high demands of the moral law of God are more clearly and emphatically presented in the New Testament than in the Old. There is no need to return to Moses for deliverance from license and antinomianism.

The following verse is so familiar that its profound theological implications are often overlooked: "For all have sinned and fall short of the glory of God" (Rom. 3:23, ASV). This statement assumes that all men are under the moral law of God and states that all have come short of its demand—which is nothing less than full conformity to the character or glory of God. This verse fully justifies Chafer's exacting definition of sin: "Sin is any want of conformity to the character of God."[2] God can be satisfied with no standard that is lower than His own perfection and glory.

How then can anyone be saved? Only by a righteousness equal to the character of God. The best human effort to obtain this standard falls infinitely short of the glory of God. But God's standard is fully met by those who receive the imputed righteousness of God: "Even the righteousness of God which is by faith of Jesus Christ unto all and upon all them that believe" (Rom. 3:22a). Those who

---

[1] Carl F. Henry, *Christian Personal Ethics*, Wm. B. Eerdmans Publishing Co., p. 353.

[2] Chafer, op. cit., II, p. 260.

believe in Christ are placed "in Christ" and thus made partakers of the very character of God. Thus it is that the gospel is called "the gospel of the glory of Christ" (2 Cor. 4:4, ASV). It is the good news by which helpless sinners are called "to the obtaining of the glory of our Lord Jesus Christ" (2 Thess. 2:14b). The believer is not only fit for heaven through the imputed righteousness of God, but he is counted as already there in his union with Christ: "And hath raised us up together, and made us sit together in heavenly places in Christ Jesus" (Eph. 2:6).

Thus the child of God has a perfect standing in Christ, though his actual conduct is often far from perfect. But his sins and imperfections are provided for by the advocacy and intercession of Christ (I John 1:6-2:2). Ability to overcome sin is imparted by the indwelling Spirit of God. "This I say then, Walk in the Spirit, and ye shall not fulfill the lust of the flesh" (Gal. 5:16).

This walk of the believer is not under any part of the Mosaic law but is to be in accord with the character of the Spirit of God. The negative precepts of the Ten Commandments have been replaced by positive demands which are as exacting as the ethics of heaven. The Christian is to "bring into captivity every thought to the obedience of Christ" (2 Cor. 10:5b). Every step of his walk is to be taken in perfect faith, "for whatsoever is not of faith is sin" (Rom. 14:23b). Mere negative or passive morality is condemned as severely as open sin: "Therefore to him that knoweth to do good, and doeth it not, to him it is sin" (Jas. 4:17). "So then because thou art lukewarm, and neither cold nor hot, I will spew thee out of my mouth" (Rev.

3:16). The Christian is always to be an imitator of Him who ceaselessly "went about doing good" (Acts 10:38b).

Such a standard of life is as high as heaven itself and has been perfectly attained by no one except Christ. But failure to attain the standard of the moral law does not change or lower its holy demands. Therefore, as theologians have recognized, the atonement of Christ includes not only His passive vicarious death on the cross for our sins, but it embraces His active obedience to all the moral law as a substitute and satisfaction for our failure to render perfect obedience. Only by such perfect fulfillment of the moral law can the sinner be saved. How thankful we should be that such fulfillment has been provided by our Savior and substitute. "For he hath made him to be sin for us, who knew no sin; that we might be made the righteousness of God in him" (2 Cor. 5:21).

In conclusion, the abrogation of the Mosaic law does not mean abrogation of the eternal moral law of God. Laws are not identical because they are based upon identical moral principles. Only a divinely instituted theocracy could enforce the Mosaic ten laws with their death penalties, and no such government exists today. The moral law of God belongs to all ages and its authority extends to all intelligent creatures whether men or angels. The essence of the moral law is conformity to the character of God. Christ alone fulfilled this law and His obedience is reckoned to those who trust in Him.

The infinitely high and holy demands of the moral law are more clearly revealed in the New Testament than in the Old. The believer's standard of conduct

is the standard of heaven (Col. 3:1). He is not without law but is under "the law of Christ" (Gal. 6:2), "the
royal law" of love (Jas. 2:8), "the law of liberty" (Jas. 2:12),
but he has nothing to do with the law of Moses (Rom.
7:4).

Chapter 7

THE TEN COMMANDMENTS RESTATED
IN THE NEW TESTAMENT

Is the Christian under the ten commandments? Those who answer this question in the affirmative point out that all of the ten commandments, except the fourth, are restated in the New Testament and therefore must apply to the Christian. But this position involves the false assumption that the moral law of God is identical with the ten commandments. The moral law is the basis of the Mosaic law, but the two should not be confused. Christians and all of God's intelligent creatures are under His eternal moral law, but only Israel was ever under the Mosaic pattern of the moral law:

> Hear, O Israel: The Lord our God is one Lord: And thou shalt love the Lord thy God with all thine heart, and with all thy soul, and with all thy might. And these words, which I command thee this day, shall be in thine heart (Deut. 6:4-6).

The simplest way to demonstrate this conclusion is to examine the Mosaic ten commandments and compare them with their restatement in the epistles of the New Testament:

1. "Thou shalt have no other gods before me" (Ex. 20:3).

The penalty for violation of this law was death. "He that sacrificeth unto any god, save unto the Lord only, he shall be utterly destroyed" (Ex. 22:20).

> Ye shall not go after other gods, of the gods of the people which are round about you; (For the Lord thy God is a jealous God among you) lest the anger of the Lord thy God be kindled against thee, and destroy thee from off the face of the earth (Deut. 6:14, 15).

This commandment is not repeated in the New Testament but the principle involved is emphatically affirmed. "For there is one God, and one mediator between God and men, the man Christ Jesus" (I Tim. 2:5). See also Acts 14:15 and James 2:19. But nowhere in the New Testament is the Mosaic penalty of physical death for violation of this law either affirmed or implied. Therefore the first commandment as Mosaic law has been annulled but the moral principle that only the true God should be worshipped and served abides forever.

2. "Thou shalt not make unto thee any graven image, or any likeness of any thing that is in heaven above, or that

is in the earth beneath, or that is in the water under the earth" (Ex. 20:4).

The penalty for violation of the second commandment was death (Deut. 27:15). After the sin of worshipping the golden calf the nation was saved from death by the intercession of Moses, but three thousand were slain who refused to give up their idolatry (Ex. 32:26-28).

The principle behind this commandment reappears in many New Testament passages (Acts 15:29; I Cor. 8:1-10; 12:2; II Cor. 6:16). John's admonition, "Little children, keep yourselves from idols" (I John 5:21), is not so much a warning against actual idols as against any thing less than full understanding and appropriation of the believer's blessings in Christ (I John 5:20). In this broader sense anything that comes between the believer and Christ is an idol. But the Mosaic death penalty for violation of the second commandment does not appear in the New Testament. Therefore, the law of Moses against idolatry has been canceled, but the principle behind this law is retained and greatly expanded.

3. "Thou shalt not take the name of the Lord thy God in vain; for the Lord will not hold him guiltless that taketh his name in vain" (Ex. 20:17).

The Mosaic penalty for transgression of this law is stated as follows:

And thou shalt speak unto the children of Israel, saying, whosoever curseth his God shall bear his sin. And he that blasphemeth the name of the Lord, he shall surely be put to death, and all the congregation shall certainly stone him: as well the stranger, as he that is born in the land, when he blasphemeth the name of the Lord shall be put to death (Lev. 24:15, 16).

In the New Testament the principle of the third commandment is expanded to include simplicity and godliness in all conversation:

Again, ye have heard that it hath been said by them of old time, Thou shalt not forswear thyself, but shalt perform unto the Lord thine oaths: But I say unto you, swear not at all: neither by heaven: for it is God's throne; Nor by the earth; for it is his footstool: neither by Jerusalem; for it is the city of the great King. Neither shalt thou swear by thy head, because thou canst not make one hair white or black. But let your communication be, Yea, yea; Nay, nay: for whatsoever is more than these cometh of evil (Matt. 5:33-37). But above all things, my brethren, swear not, neither by heaven, neither by the earth, neither by an other oath: but let your yea be yea; and your nay, nay; lest ye fall into condemnation (James 5:12).

Note that there is no parallel for the Old Testament death penalty. It must be concluded that the third Mosaic law has been done away but it must be recognized that the principle upon which it was based is as timeless as the holiness of God.

4. "Remember the Sabbath day, to keep it holy" (Ex. 20:8).

The Jewish Sabbath was the last day of the week or Saturday. The fourth commandment is nowhere reaffirmed as binding for the new age of grace. As a matter of fact, the Jewish Sabbath is specifically mentioned as one of the ordinances which is blotted out by the cross.

> Blotting out the handwriting of ordinances that was against us, which was contrary to us, and took it out of the way, nailing it to his cross; And having spoiled principalities and powers, he made a shew of them openly, triumphing over them in it. Let no man therefore judge you in meat, or in drink, or in respect of an holyday, or of the new moon, or of the sabbath days: (Col. 2:14-16).

The principle that one day out of seven belongs in a special way to God is reembodied in the Christian's observance of the first day of the week as the Lord's day. No specific instruction instituted this new day but its observance seems to have arisen spontaneously in honor and recognition of the resurrection of Christ. The claim of the Seventh Day Adventists that the pope changed the clay from Saturday to Sunday in 321 A.D. will not bear serious investigation. There was no pope in 321 A.D. and history shows that Christians observed the first day from apostolic times.

The penalty for violation of the Mosaic Sabbath law was death. The man found gathering sticks on the Sabbath day was stoned to death by the explicit instructions of the Lord.

> And while the children of Israel were in the wilderness, they found a man that gathered sticks upon the

sabbath day. And they that found him gathering sticks brought him unto Moses and Aaron, and unto all the congregation. And they put him in ward, because it was not declared what should be done to him. And the Lord said unto Moses, The man shall be surely put to death: all the congregation shall stone him with stones without the camp. And all the congregation brought him without the camp and stoned him with stones, and he died; as the Lord commanded Moses (Num. 15:32-36).

Those who think they are under the Mosaic Sabbath law should realize the awfulness of their position. To maintain that the Sabbath law abides but its penalties are canceled is an untenable position. The passage which teaches redemption from the curse of the law explains that this is accomplished by deliverance from the law itself (Gal. 3:10-25).

Writers who speak of the Mosaic ten commandments as the "inexorable law of God" are embarrassed to find themselves in agreement with the Seventh Day Adventist position. When this is discovered they try to extricate themselves with the historical argument alone to justify observance of the first day of the week. This leaves the Adventists with the best of the debate. How much better it is to recognize the clear teaching of Scripture that the Mosaic law was a temporary institution "added" to the Abrahamic covenant "till" the seed should come (Gal. 3:17-19). Now all of the law is done away but its moral principle that part of man's time should be specially set apart for the worship and service of God is perpetuated in the observance of the first day of the week. Neither the Jewish Sabbath nor the Lord's Day was ever intended to detract from the broader moral truth that all of the believer's time and service belong to God. "One man esteemeth one day above another: another esteemeth every day alike. Let every man be fully persuaded in his own mind" (Rom. 14:5).

5. "Honor thy father and thy mother: that thy days may be long upon the land which the Lord thy God giveth thee" (Ex. 20:12).

The penalty for the overt violation of the fifth commandment was death. "And he that smiteth his father, or his mother, shall be surely put to death" (Ex. 21:15). "And he that curseth his father, or his mother, shall surely be put to death" (Ex. 21:17). "Cursed be he that setteth light by his father or his mother" (Deut. 27:16a). The rebellious son, who refused all correction, was to be stoned to death by the elders of the city (Deut. 21:18-21).

In his argument with the Pharisees Christ upheld this law with its full Mosaic penalty.

> But he answered and said unto them, Why do ye also transgress the commandment of God by your tradition? For God commanded, saying, Honor thy father and mother: and He that curseth father or mother, let him die the death (Matt. 15:3, 4).

> Christ lived under the Mosaic law and upheld its authority. Many overlook the fact that the age of Mosaic law ended only with the death of Christ (Col.

2:14); not with his birth or during his ministry. Some point triumphantly to the restatement of the fifth commandment in Ephesians as conclusive proof that the Mosaic law is still binding.

Children, obey your parents in the Lord: for this is right. Honor thy father and mother; which is the first commandment with promise; That it may be well with thee, and thou mayest live long on the earth (Eph. 6:1-3).

It is significant that they overlook our Lord's reference to this command in Matt. 15:3, 4. Why? Doubtless because Christ recognized that this law, as Mosaic legislation, could not be separated from its death penalty. But in Ephesians the penalty is omitted and nowhere is it reinstated for this age of grace. It should also be noted that the promise of long life in the land of Palestine as a reward for obedience is changed to a promise of long life on the earth—thus making the reward of universal application for the new age.

It is thus evident that the fifth commandment, as Mosaic legislation, has been canceled, but its moral principle is emphatically reaffirmed under grace and belongs to every dispensation.

6. "Thou shalt not kill" (Ex. 20:13).

The Mosaic penalty for murder was death. "He that smiteth a man, so that he die, shall be surely put to death" (Ex. 21:12). However, the Mosaic law distinguished between manslaughter and murder by providing mercy for manslaughter in the cities of refuge (Num. 35). But careless manslaughter was punishable by death. If an ox killed a man, and it was known that the ox was dangerous and safeguards had been neglected, the owner was to be put to death (Ex. 21:29).

The death penalty for murder was instituted long before the time of Moses (Gen. 9:5, 6). The sinfulness of murder is not only recognized in the New Testament, but it is declared that hatred is incipient murder. "Whosoever hateth his brother is a murderer: and ye know that no murderer hath eternal life abiding in him" (I John 3:15).

That the Christian is not under Mosaic legislation concerning murder and manslaughter involves no more problem or antinomianism than the evident truth that the citizen of Michigan is not under the laws against homicide of the State of Illinois. This is far from a theoretical distinction since Illinois has capital punishment and Michigan does not.

7. "Thou shalt not commit adultery" (Ex. 20:14).

Death was the Mosaic penalty for both parties involved in violation of this command. "And the man that committeth adultery with his neighbor's wife, the adulterer and the adulteress shall surely be put to death" (Lev. 20:10).

Long before the time of Moses the cities of Sodom and Gomorrah were destroyed for wholesale violation of the moral principle of this law. Christ taught that lustful desire was incipient adultery:

> Ye have heard that it was said by them of old time,
> Thou shalt not commit adultery: But I say unto you,
> That whosoever looketh on a woman to lust after her
> hath committed adultery with her already in his heart
> (Matt. 5:27, 28).

Surely no one would argue that we are under Mosaic legislation regarding adultery. In contrast to the Mosaic death penalty, modern churches debate whether or not the adulterer should be elected to church membership and even to hold church offices.

Under grace the moral law of God against adultery and all forms of impurity is enforced, not by appeal to a death sentence—but by reminding the believer that he is united to Christ and indwelt by the Spirit of God:

> Flee fornication. Every sin that a man doeth is without
> the body; but he that committeth fornication sinneth
> against his own body. What? know ye not that your
> body is the temple of the Holy Ghost which is in you,
> which ye have of God, and ye are not your own? For
> ye are bought with a price: therefore glorify God in
> your body, and in your spirit, which are God's (I Cor.
> 6:18-20).

That this is not the same as Mosaic law should be self-evident.

8. "Thou shalt not steal" (Ex. 20:15).

For stealing an ox or a sheep the penalties were respectively five fold and four fold restoration (Ex. 22:1). For stealing a man, or kidnapping, the penalty of the Mosaic law was death: "And he that stealeth a man, and selleth him, or if he be found in his hand, he shall surely be put to death" (Ex. 21:16).

In the New Testament the moral law against larceny appears in a beautiful framework of grace: "Let him that stole steal no more: but rather let him labour, working with his hands the thing which is good, that he may have to give to him that needeth" (Eph. 4:28). The convert, who was formerly a thief, is to work at legitimate labor in order to have something to give to the needy, and thus lessen the temptation of the poor to steal. As transformed in the New Testament, the negative law against stealing becomes a gracious principle of Christian stewardship. The Christian is stealing if he is not a good giver. Surely it can be recognized that this is not Mosaic legislation.

9. "Thou shalt not bear false witness against thy neighbour" (Ex. 20:16).

The Mosaic penalties for false witnessing are stated thus:

> If a false witness rise up against any man to testify against him that which is wrong. . . . Then shall ye do unto him, as he had thought to have done unto his brother: so shalt thou put the evil away from among you . . . And thine eye shall not pity; but life shall go for life, eye for eye, tooth for tooth, hand for hand, foot for foot (Deut. 19:16, 19, 21).

Thus the ninth commandment was to be enforced by exact and severe penalties.

The moral principle of this commandment reappears in the New Testament in an entirely different setting: "Lie not one to another, seeing that ye have put off the old man with his deeds; and have put on the new man, which is renewed in knowledge after the image of him that created him" (Col. 3:9, 10). Here the appeal for honesty is not based upon the fear of penalty, but upon the incongruity of doing anything so unbecoming to the believer's new nature in Christ. This is not Mosaic law but an example of what it means to be "inlawed to Christ," which is the literal meaning of "under the law to Christ" in I Cor. 9:21.

10. "Thou shalt not covet" (Ex. 20:17a).

For obvious reasons the Mosaic law states no penalty for covetousness in thought only. However, if covetousness found expression in stealing, adultery, or other sins—the Mosaic penalty for the particular sin was applied. Thus death could be the indirect penalty for some manifestations of covetousness.

The moral principle of the tenth commandment reappears in the New Testament in a setting of grace: "But fornication, and all uncleanness, or covetousness, let it not be once named among you, as becometh saints" (Eph. 5:3). The appeal for separation from all sin, including covetousness, is based upon the character of the saints; not upon fear of the law.

The death penalty seems to be manditory for violation of the first three commandments. The penalty could be death for certain overt violations of each of the remaining seven commandments. No wonder the apostle Paul calls the Mosaic ten commandments "the ministration of death, written and engraven in stones" (II Cor. 3:7).

In conclusion, it has been noted that none of the ten commandments reappear in the New Testament for this age of grace as Mosaic legislation. All of the moral principles of the ten laws do reappear in the New Testament in a framework of grace. The Christian is not under "the ministration of death, written and engraven in stones," but he is under all the moral principles on those stones restated for this economy of grace. He is under the eternal moral law of God which demands far more than the ten commandments. It calls for nothing less than conformity to the character of God. This is as far from antinomianism as heaven is far above the earth.

As a motorist enters a certain residential section of Detroit he sees this sign: "Good citizens drive 25 miles per hour." This is different from the usual traffic warning which is something like the following: "Speed limit, 30 miles, radar controlled." The first is a gracious suggestion while the second is law. The eternal moral laws of God were embodied in a code of legislation by Moses with fitting penalties for every violation. Under grace the same moral principles appear but in a setting of grace that might be paraphrased as follows: "Good citizens of heaven live by the manners of heaven." This is almost exactly what Paul says:

Brethren, be ye imitators together of me, and mark
them that so walk even as ye have us for an example . .
. For our citizenship is in heaven: whence also we wait
for a Saviour, the Lord Jesus Christ (Phil. 3:17, 20 R.V.).

The believer is not under the ten commandments, "the
ministration of death" which the children of Israel "could
not endure" (II Cor. 3:7; Heb. 12:20). "Wherefore we
receiving a kingdom which cannot be moved, let us have
(hold fast to) grace, whereby we may serve God acceptably
with reverence and godly fear" (Heb. 12:28).

Chapter 8

THE PROBLEM PASSAGES

There are certain portions of Scripture commonly cited to prove that the Mosaic law has not been done away. In dealing with these problem passages there are some general principles of interpretation to be observed.

The first is that: "Truth must accord with truth; and statements of truth apparently discrepant can be harmonized if the facts are known."[1] It cannot be true that the Mosaic law has been abrogated and abolished and at the same time remain in force. The passages which seem to teach the Mosaic law is still in effect must have some other explanation.

Another principle is that: "Obscure passages must give right of way to clear passages."[2] Granted that there are some difficult passages which seem to teach Mosaic legalism, these should be interpreted in harmony with the book of Galatians and with the numerous other portions

---

[1] Rollin T. Chafer, *The Science of Biblical Hermeneutics*, Dallas Seminary Press, p. 30.

[2] Bernard Ramm, *Protestant Biblical Interpretation*, W. A. Wilde Co., p. 95.

of the New Testament which clearly teach freedom from the law.

Again, some of the difficult passages can be explained by observing the sense in which the term "law" is used. As previously noted, this word has several meanings in the Bible and does not always refer to the Mosaic law.

Also clear dispensational distinctions should be observed. Here we are not concerned with the current debate over the details of dispensationalism, but only with the difference between the Mosaic economy and this church age, regardless of what titles may be preferred for these evident divisions of Bible history. Even the most ardent antidispensationalists recognize at least two dispensations in the Bible. Thus R. B. Kuiper acknowledges:

> In accordance with the divine plan of history the old dispensation belongs to the irrevocable past. In the new dispensation no preacher may be satisfied to occupy the standpoint of the old. A sermon on an Old Testament text must always be a New Testament sermon.[3]

Boettner is severely critical of dispensationalism but concedes there are two dispensations:

> Hence there are two, and only two, great divisions, or dispensations, in God's dealings with men—that of the Old Covenant, and that of the New Covenant, or as we are more accustomed to refer to them, that of the Old Testament, and that of the New Testament.[4]

---

[3] N. B. Stonehouse and Paul Woolley, *The Infallible Word*, Wm. B. Eerdmans Publishing Co., p. 228.
[4] Loraine Boettner, *The Millennium*, The Presbyterian and Reformed Publishing Company, p. 312.

Thus to quote passages from the Gospels, which apply to the period before the cross, to prove the Mosaic law is still in effect is to misunderstand the problem entirely. Such citations only prove that the Mosaic law was in effect before it was abrogated. This no one denies but those who reject the New Testament. It was not the birth of Christ but His cross that marked the end of the Mosaic economy: "Christ hath redeemed us from the curse of the law, being made a curse for us: for it is written, Cursed is every one that hangeth on a tree" (Gal. 3:13).

In addition the differences and the similarities between the eternal moral law of God and the Mosaic law should be understood. This is the area of greatest confusion. The moral law of God is common to all dispensations. The Mosaic framework of the moral law was temporary and has been abrogated. The similarities between the Mosaic ten commandments and their restatement for the church age does not prove we are under the Mosaic law any more than it proves we are under the economy of the garden of Eden. It only proves that the moral law is eternal.

When the difficult passages are examined in the light of these foregoing principles, the problems can be solved.

The following are the most frequently cited verses as supposed proof of obligation to the Mosaic law:

1. Think not that I am come to destroy the law, or the prophets: I am not come to destroy, but to fulfil. For verily I say unto you, Till heaven and earth pass, one jot or one tittle shall in no wise pass from the law, till all be fulfilled. Whosoever therefore shall break one of these least commandments, and shall teach men so, he

shall be called the least in the kingdom of heaven: but whosoever shall do and teach them, the same shall be called great in the kingdom of heaven (Matt. 5:17-19).

Here Christ is defending the authority of the Old Testament against both unbelief and antinomianism. He is saying that all of its prophecies will be fulfilled and that all of its precepts are to be obeyed. The expression, "the law or the prophets" doubtless refers to the entire Old Testament.

> It is highly probable that, when Jesus says "the law or the prophets," He denotes by these two designations the whole of the Old Testament, the law denoting what we know as the Pentateuch and the prophets the rest of the Old Testament.[5]

This probability is made quite certain by the explanations the risen Christ gave to His disciples of the way in which His death and resurrection had fulfilled all the Scriptures: "And beginning at Moses and all the prophets, he expounded unto them in all the scriptures the things concerning himself" (Luke 24:27).

> And he said unto them, These are the words which I spake unto you, while I was yet with you, that all things must be fulfilled, which were written in the law of Moses, and in the prophets, and in the psalms, concerning me (Luke 24:44).

---

[5] Stonehouse and Woolley, op. cit., p. 20.

If taken by itself, Matt. 5:19 might seem to teach the permanent validity of the entire Mosaic system. That this is not the meaning is agreed by all. Since all interpreters agree that some part or parts of the Mosaic economy were to pass away this verse loses its force as an argument for any degree of Mosaic legalism. Stevens' comment on this passage is to the point:

> He does not, therefore, say that no part of this system shall ever pass away (as it has done, and that, too, in consequence of his own teaching), but that no part of it shall escape the process of fulfillment; that it shall not pass away till, having served its providential purpose, it is fulfilled in the gospel.[6]

The Old Testament economy is abrogated by way of fulfillment, not by way of destruction. All the permanent moral precepts of the law are preserved and embodied in Christianity.

The way in which Christ fulfilled the Mosaic law may be briefly summarized as follows: (1) He was born under the Mosaic law and fulfilled its requirements in his personal life (Gal. 4:4, John 8:45, Matt. 17:5). (2) He fulfilled the law by clarifying and elevating its moral truths. This is seen in the context of the passage under discussion, where the deeper and absolute principles of morality are described in contrast to the letter of the Mosaic law or to the rabbinical misunderstandings of the law. (3) He fulfilled the promises and types of the law which pointed to a coming Redeemer (Rom. 15:8, 9; Heb. 9:11-10:22). (4) He fulfilled the law

---

[6] Stevens, op. cit., p. 19.

by bearing its curse and penalty and thus manifest the basis for saving both Jews and Gentiles who believe (Gal. 3:10-14, Rom. 3:25, 26). (5) He fulfilled the law by his death in providing His blood for a new covenant of grace to supercede the old covenant of Moses (Heb. 8:6-13). The law of Moses is thus fulfilled in the new and higher "law of Christ," obedience to which is made possible by the indwelling Spirit (Gal. 6:2; 5:17, 22).

It should be remembered that Jeremiah prophesied that the old covenant was to be superceded by a new covenant which would be characterized by the gracious forgiveness of God and the willing obedience of His people:

> Behold, the days come, saith the Lord, that I will make a new covenant with the house of Israel, and with the house of Judah: Not according to the covenant that I made with their fathers in the day that I took them by the hand to bring them out of the land of Egypt; which my covenant they brake, although I was an husband unto them, saith the Lord: But this shall be the covenant that I will make with the house of Israel; After those days, saith the Lord, I will put my law in their inward parts, and write it in their hearts; and will be their God, and they shall be my people. And they shall teach no more every man his neighbour, and every man his brother, saying, Know the Lord: for they shall all know me, from the least of them unto the greatest of them, saith the Lord: for I will forgive their iniquity, and I will remember their sin no more. Thus saith the Lord, which giveth the sun for a light by day, and the ordinances of the moon and of the stars for a light by night, which divideth the sea when the waves thereof

roar; The Lord of hosts is his name; If those ordinances depart from before me, saith the Lord, then the seed of Israel also shall cease from being a nation before me for ever. Thus saith the Lord; if heaven above can be measured, and the foundations of the earth searched out beneath, I will cast off all the seed of Israel for all that they have done, saith the Lord (Jer. 31:31-37).

Here God calls upon the very ordinances of heaven and earth to witness to the certainty of this promise of future blessing through a new covenant. Therefore, the very inviolability of "the law and the prophets" demands the passing away of the old economy and the institution of the new age of "grace and truth" (John 1:17).

2. "Do we then make the law of none effect through faith? God forbid: nay, we establish the law" (Rom. 3:31 R.V.).

If this verse is studied in the light of its context it presents no serious difficulty. Paul has shown in Rom. 3:19, 20, that the law was never intended for salvation, but only as a tutor to lead to faith. The next few verses do not teach that justification by faith is a new way of salvation but only that the basis upon which God justifies the ungodly has now been clearly revealed:

But now apart from the law a righteousness of God hath been manifested, being witnessed by the law and the prophets; even the righteousness of God through faith in Jesus Christ unto all them that believe; for there is no distinction; for all have sinned, and fall short of the glory of God; being justified freely by his grace through the redemption that is in Christ Jesus: whom God set forth to be a propitiation, through faith in his blood, to show his righteousness at this present season: that he might himself be just, and the justifier of him that hath faith in Jesus (Rom. 3:21-26 R.V.).

Does God's plan of justification by faith alone make the law of none effect? No. The very purpose of the law is thus fully realized which is that of a tutor to point to Christ and the necessity of grace (Rom. 3:19, 20; Gal. 5:24, 25). This way of salvation in the old order is confirmed and illustrated in the cases of Abraham and David in Romans 4.

Some believe that the reference in Rom. 3:31 is not specifically to the Mosaic law because the article does not appear before the word "law" in this verse. In this case the reference would be to law or morality in general and the meaning would be that the highest morality is established by those who are justified by faith and walk by the Spirit as more fully explained in the subsequent chapters.

> 3. For what the law could not do, in that it was weak through the flesh, God sending his own Son in the likeness of sinful flesh, and for sin, condemned sin in the flesh: That the righteousness of the law might be fulfilled in us, who walk not after the flesh, but after the Spirit (Rom. 8:3, 4).

From this passage it is argued that if "the righteousness of the law" must be fulfilled in us, then we are under the Mosaic law. In answer it is first noted that Paul has not so soon forgotten and contradicted what he had just written in Romans 6:14 and 7:1-7 about freedom from the law. In fact the very statement under consideration teaches clearly that victory over sin is impossible of attainment on a legal basis but only on the new principle of walking by the Spirit. "The righteousness of the law" refers to the essential moral principles embodied in the law, or to what we have called the eternal moral law of God. Enoch fulfilled "the righteousness of the law" without ever hearing of Moses. "The righteousness of the law" of Romans 8:4 is produced by walking after the Spirit and is thus the exact equivalent of "the fruit of the Spirit" of Gal. 5:22, 23. Far from teaching Mosaic legalism, Romans 8:3, 4 is one of the emphatic New Testament refutations of the common error that the law can produce righteousness.

> 4. Owe no man anything, save to love one another: for he that loveth his neighbor hath fulfilled the law. For this, Thou shalt not commit adultery, Thou shalt not kill, Thou shalt not steal, Thou shalt not covet, and if there be any other commandment, it is summed up in this word, namely, Thou shalt love thy neighbor as thyself. Love worketh no ill to his neighbor: love therefore is the fulfilling of the law (Rom. 13:8-10).

This passage is often cited to show that the ten commandments are the rule of life for the believer of this dispensation. Does not Paul quote the second table of the law and refer to "any other commandment?" Surely this proves the ten commandments are the rule of life for the Christian.

Actually Paul is proving the opposite of the legalist's conclusion. He is refuting the naive but common assumption that all morality stands or falls with the Mosaic law. He is showing that the law of love fulfills all the righteous demands of the Mosaic law and thus supercedes it. An economy of love is not the same as an economy of law, although the essential moral principles are the same in both. The Christian is under the law of love and therefore not under the law of Moses. Five of the ten commandments are quoted by Paul, not to prove that the Christian is under Mosaic law, but to show that these moral principles are fulfilled in a higher rule of life.

It will doubtless be pointed out that the saying, "Thou shalt love thy neighbor as thyself," is a quotation from Lev. 19:18, and is, therefore a part of the law. True; but this only shows that the economy of law was also to be an economy of love. Perfect love to both God and man is the essence of the eternal moral law of God and is demanded of all intelligent creatures in every age. But the law of love, in the Mosaic age, did not cancel the several hundred specific statutes of that economy. Dispensationally the Jews were as children still under the discipline and bondage of the rules of childhood as represented by the law. Now, through Christ, believers have been delivered from the law to receive a position of adult sons in the family of God.

> Even so we, when we were children, were in bondage under the elements of the world: But when the fulness of the time was come, God sent forth his Son, made of a woman, made under the law, To redeem them that were under the law, that we might receive the adoption of

sons. And because ye are sons, God hath sent forth the
Spirit of his Son into your hearts, crying, Abba, Father.
Wherefore thou art no more a servant, but a son; and if
a son, then an heir of God through Christ (Gal. 4:3-7).

God now trusts His children to behave as adult sons
from the inward motive of love without the bondage of a
legal system.

It should be noted that the law of love comprehends
and teaches only the essential principles of the eternal
moral law of God as written in the hearts of all men.

For when the Gentiles, which have not the law, do by
nature the things contained in the law, these, having
not the law, are a law unto themselves: Which shew the
work of the law written in their hearts, their conscience
also bearing witness, and their thoughts the mean while
accusing or else excusing one another; (Rom. 2:14, 15).

But the law of love does not teach the details of the
Mosaic system. It does not teach it is wrong to gather sticks
on Saturday, or that all males should be circumcised, or
that God should be worshipped at Jerusalem with animal
sacrifices. Love comprehends the essence of the moral law,
but not the many specific non-moral details of the Mosaic
law. Therefore, the teaching of Rom. 13:8-10 is that the
law of love has delivered us from the Mosaic law. Only this
conclusion is in harmony with what Paul had previously
written in Romans about freedom from the entire Mosaic
system (Rom. 6:14-7:7).

The passage under discussion is concluded with this pertinent statement: ". . . love is the fulfilling of the law" (Rom. 13:10b). Literally this may be translated "love is 'pleroma'—fullness, fulfillment, or completion of law." The legislature does not need to pass laws to govern a normal mother's many obligations to her child. All such obligations, plus ten thousand kindnesses that lie outside the realm of duty, are embraced in a mother's love. John writes, "Every one that doeth sin doeth also lawlessness; and sin is lawlessness" (I John 3:4 R.V.). Sin is lawlessness but love is "fullness of law." But the "fullness of law" that results from love is clearly fullness of the eternal moral law of God—not fullness of the Mosaic law.

> 5. For brethren, ye have been called unto liberty; only use not liberty for an occasion to the flesh, but by love serve one another. For all the law is fulfilled in one word, even in this: Thou shalt love thy neighbor as thyself (Gal. 5:13, 14).

The teaching of these verses is identical with Rom. 13:8-10, and therefore the same explanations apply. The law of love binds the believer to all obligation but not to Mosaic legislation.

> 6. And hereby we do know that we know him, if we keep his commandments. He that saith, I know him, and keepeth not his commandments, is a liar, and the truth is not in him. But whoso keepeth his word, in him verily is the love of God perfected: hereby know we that we are in him (I John 2:3-5). See also I John 5:3 and II John 5, 6.

It ought to be unnecessary to point out that the expression, "his commandments," as used by John, has no reference to the Mosaic commandments but refers rather to the precepts of Christ, and especially to his all embracing command concerning love. In the upper room discourse Christ said, "A new commandment I give unto you, That ye love one another; as I have loved you, that ye also love one another" (John 13:34). The command to love was not new, but here it is made new by the addition of the requirement that it should be as boundless and infinite as the love of Christ to us. Christ also taught that love to Him would be manifest in keeping His commandments (John 14:21-23). John is but repeating and emphasizing the teaching of the Lord. The love that grace enjoins will not produce lawlessness but obedience to the highest commands of Christ. His commandments, which "are not grievous," (I John 5:3), should not be confused with the thunders of Sinai which the children of Israel "could not endure" (Heb. 12:20a).

> 7. But be ye doers of the word, and not hearers only, deceiving your own selves. For if any be a hearer of the word, and not a doer, he is like unto a man beholding his natural face in a glass: For he beholdeth himself, and goeth his way, and straightway forgetteth what manner of man he was. But whoso looketh unto the perfect law of liberty, and continueth therein, he being not a forgetful hearer but a doer of the work, this man shall be blessed in his deed (James 1:22-25).

If ye fulfil the royal law according to the scripture, Thou shalt love thy neighbour as thyself, ye do well: But if ye have respect to persons, ye commit sin, and are convinced of the law as transgressors. For whosoever shall keep the whole law, and yet offend in one point, he is guilty of all. For he that said, Do not commit adultery, said also, Do not kill. Now if thou commit no adultery, yet if thou kill, thou are become a transgressor of the law. So speak ye, and so do, as they that shall be judged by the law of liberty (James 2:8-12).

The author of these verses is the same James who summarized the verdict of the council at Jerusalem that the Gentiles were not under the law of Moses (Acts 15:13-29). Implicit in this decision was Peter's conclusion that the gift of the Holy Spirit had freed the Jews as well as the Gentiles from the yoke of the law (Acts 15:7-11). The believer in inspiration will approach the book of James with the conviction that it does not contradict Acts 15 or any other part of the New Testament which teaches freedom from the law of Moses.

The verses quoted from the first chapter of James show that he uses the word "law" as the equivalent of the Word of God. The Old Testament was the only Bible of the early Christians, but now it was understood in the light of the cross and the new covenant. James describes Christianity as the highest ethical life in terms of law—but law from which all legalism has been omitted. He calls the law of love "the royal law" because it is king of all laws and embraces all other obligations to our fellow men. He calls it again "the law of liberty" because he who loves does what he pleases but he pleases to do the will of God. Augustine's statement, "Love, and do as you please" is sound doctrine as long as the word "love" is used with its New Testament implications. The Christian is to be judged by "the law of liberty" and therefore he is under it and not under the law of Moses.

But James says that "whosoever shall keep the whole law and yet offend in one point, he is guilty of all," and then he refers to two of the ten commandments. Does this not indicate obligation to the Mosaic system? The answer is that he uses the expression "whole law" to describe the total ethical demands of the Scriptures—not the whole law of Moses. The thrust of his argument is that respect of persons violates the law of love. The legalist is always concerned with the technicalities of the law—never with the law of love. He worries about circumcision, and meat and drink, and the sabbath (Gal. 1-6; Col. 2:16), but has to be reminded of the essence of all divine law (Gal. 5:13, 14). If the legalist began with the law of love his legalism would vanish.

As if to forestall any inference that he refers to the Mosaic economy, James closes the section under discussion by pointing out that the believer is to be judged by "the law of liberty." As already noted, this places the Christian squarely under grace.

Finally, it should be observed that James' description of "pure religion" is in accord with the highest ethical principles of the new dispensation.

> If any man among you seem to be religious, and
> bridleth, not his tongue, but deceiveth his own heart,

this man's religion is vain. Pure religion and undefiled before God and the Father is this, To visit the fatherless and widows in their affliction, and to keep himself unspotted from the world (James 1:26, 27).

James leaves no loophole for conduct lower than the standards of heaven by declaring that failure to perform any known good is sin (James 4:17). Such high demands for personal purity and active charity call for the work of the Spirit, and exclude the possibility that Paul and James are in disagreement.

In this chapter the passages most frequently used to bolster Mosaic legalism have been examined and explained in harmony with grace and with the clear New Testament teaching that all the Mosaic system has been abolished. The few additional passages either fall in the same categories with those already answered or they can be harmonized by use of the accepted hermeneutical principles mentioned at the beginning of the chapter. The entire New Testament is in accord with the conclusion that the new robe of grace needs no patching from the old garment of Mosaic law.

Chapter 9

CONCLUSION

Our study of law and grace began with an emphasis upon the practice of the deeper spiritual life under grace. It was shown that though evangelicals differ over the doctrinal background of sanctification they are in general agreement that holiness is the result of the simple practice of walking with the Lord. A wide variety of devotional and spiritual life books were quoted to show this agreement. The reader will find help and blessing in rereading chapter one several times. In addition we recommend the purchase and careful study of the spiritual life books which have been quoted and are listed in the bibliography. Every Christian should be a specialist in spirituality.

Chapters two and three show the confusion that exists in the area of law and grace, and that the primary cause of this confusion is the failure to distinguish between the eternal moral law of God and the Mosaic economy. When many say we are under the Mosaic ten commandments they really mean we are under the eternal moral law of God. But to avoid legalism and confusion the New Testament teaching of complete freedom from the Mosaic system must be acknowledged. No antinomianism is involved, as the moral law of God remains.

Chapter four shows that the Scriptures treat the Mosaic laws as a unit which cannot be separated into parts that are abolished and parts that remain. Chapter five presents the clear New Testament teaching that the entire Mosaic system, including the ten commandments, has been done away.

Chapter six is a brief study of the heavenly standard of the moral law. Those who may have misgivings that grace implies license will be helped by realizing that the standard of the moral law is as high as the character of God.

Chapter seven deals with the restatement of the ten commandments in the New Testament and shows that they are not reaffirmed as Mosaic laws but as grace principles and elements of the eternal moral law of God. The Christian is not under "the ministration of death" of Exodus 20, but is under the "law of love" of I Cor. 13. The constraint of love needs none of the fearful penalties of the Mosaic law to guide the believer's feet on the path of obedience.

Chapter eight is a study of the passages which are thought by some to teach obligation to the Mosaic system. It is shown that such passages are in harmony with the clear and positive Scriptures which teach complete freedom from the Mosaic law.

"Wherefore we receiving a kingdom which cannot be moved, let us have (hold fast to) grace, whereby we may serve God acceptably with reverence and godly fear" (Heb. 12:28).

BIBLIOGRAPHY OF BOOKS
ON THE SPIRITUAL LIFE

Barabas, Steven, *So Great Salvation*, Fleming H. Revell Company.

Barnhouse, Donald Grey, *God's Methods for Holy Living*, Eternity Book Service.

Bro. Lawrence, *The Practice of the Presence of God*, Fleming H. Revell Company.

Chafer, Lewis Sperry, *He That Is Spiritual*, Dunham Publishing Company.

Elliot, Elisabeth, *Shadow of the Almighty*, Harper & Brothers Publishers.

Finney, Charles G., *Sanctification*, Christian Literature Crusade.

Fordsham, Stanley, *The Spirit Filled Life*, Wm. B. Eerdmans Publishing Company.

Grubb, Norman, *The Liberating Secret*, Christian Literature Crusade.

Harrison, Norman B., *New Testament Living*, The Harrison Service.

Hession, Roy and Revel, *We Would See Jesus*, Christian Literature Crusade.

Hopkins, Evan, *The Law of Liberty in the Spiritual Life*, the American Rights are Held by the Sunday School Times.

Huegel, F. J., *Bone of His Bone*, Zondervan Publishing House.

Kramer, Alice Bishop and Albert Ludlow, *The Life In The Vine*, Fleming H. Revell Company.

Laubach, Frank C., *Letters by a Modern Mystic*, Fleming H. Revell Company.

Mantle, Gregory J., *Beyond Humiliation*, Used by permission of Moody Bible Institute, Moody Press, 820 N. LaSalle Street, Chicago, Illinois.

Meyer, F. B., *Meet For the Master's Use*, Moody Press.

Monod, Theodore, *Looking unto Jesus*, Box 351 Athens, Georgia.

Palmer, Orson R., *Deliverance from the Penalty and Power of Sin*, Moody Press.

Paxson, Ruth, *Rivers of Living Waters*, Moody Press.

Sanders, Oswald J., *Christ Indwelling and Enthroned*, Christian Literature Crusade.

Smith, Hannah W., *The Christian's Secret of a Happy Life*, Fleming H. Revell Company.

Taylor, Dr. and Mrs. Howard, *Hudson Taylor's Spiritual Secret*, China Inland Mission.

Tozer, A. W., *The Divine Conquest*, Fleming H. Revell Company.

Tozer, A. W., *The Pursuit of God*, Christian Publications Inc.

Unger, Merrill F., *Pathways to Power*, Zondervan Publishing House.

Unkown Author, *How to Live a Victorious Christian Life*, Zondervan Publishing House.

Whittle, D. W., *Life, Warfare, and Victory*, Moody Press.

CPSIA information can be obtained
at www.ICGtesting.com
Printed in the USA
BVHW070745110620
581224BV00003B/144